D0284744

101
MOST
POWERFUL
PROVERBS
IN THE
BIBLE

101 MOST POWERFUL PROVERBS IN THE BIBLE

J. Stephen Lang

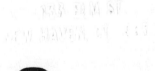

WARNER
Faith

A Division of AOL Time Warner Book Group

Published in association with the literary agency of Alive Communications, Inc., 7680 Goddard Street, Suite 200, Colorado Springs, CO 80920.

Unless otherwise noted, Scripture quotations are from The Holy Bible, English Standard Version, copyright © 2001 by Crossway Bibles, a division of Good News Publishers. Used by permission. All rights reserved.

Scripture quotations noted NIV are from the HOLY BIBLE: NEW INTERNATIONAL VERSION®. Copyright © 1973, 1978, 1984 by International Bible Society. Used by permission of Zondervan Bible Publishers. All rights reserved.

Scripture quotations noted KJV are from the KING JAMES VERSION.

Visit our website at www.twbookmark.com

⚙ WARNER*Faith* A Division of AOL Time Warner Book Group

Warner Faith is a trademark of Warner Books Inc.

Printed in the United States of America

First Warner Books Printing: March 2003

10 9 8 7 6 5 4 3 2 1

Library of Congress Cataloging-in-Publication Data

101 most powerful Proverbs in the Bible / J. Stephen Lang, Steve Rabey, and Lois Rabey, general editors.
    p. cm.
    ISBN 0-446-53215-0
    1. Bible. O.T. Proverbs—Criticism, interpretation, etc. I. Title: One hundred and one most powerful Proverbs in the Bible. II. Title: One hundred one most powerful Proverbs in the Bible. III. Lang, J. Stephen. IV. Rabey, Steve. V. Rabey, Lois Mowday.

BS1465.52.A15 2004
223'.706—dc22   2003057600

Contents

CONTENTS

General Editors' Preface

There are thousands of verses in the Bible. How can we find those verses containing the divine wisdom and guidance that will help us grow spiritually and live more faithfully? This book and others in the 101 Most Powerful series will help you find and unlock powerful passages of Scripture that inspire, comfort and challenge.

101 Most Powerful Prayers in the Bible helps us open our hearts to God by showing us how earlier saints and sinners prayed.

101 Most Powerful Promises in the Bible brings together those passages that convey God's boundless and eternal love for his creation and his creatures.

And *101 Most Powerful Verses in the Bible* provides a treasury of divine insight gathered from nearly every book of the Old and New Testaments.

101 Most Powerful Proverbs in the Bible will enable us to apply God's timeless truths to many of the messy details of daily life.

We believe J. Stephen Lang is the ideal author to unlock the timeless wisdom found in Solomon's ancient proverbs. He has written many articles for major magazines. He is a former book editor, and himself the author of more than twenty books.

Stephen can extract and explain the essence of even the most obscure biblical passages, and he writes with an energy and concreteness that fits well with the poetic and practical nature of the Book of Proverbs.

This and the other books in this series will never replace the Bible, but we do hope they will help you grasp its powerful and life-changing lessons and better utilize its wisdom in your life.

Steve and Lois Rabey

Introduction:
The Book of Reminders

The wise folk of the world understand a basic truth about wisdom: it is not new. It is all "old stuff" that thousands of years of human beings living on God's earth have tested. There is no "new wisdom," for human nature has not changed one iota.

When we read or hear wise sayings, we are hearing only "reminders" of what our ancestors knew. We need to be reminded for the same reason our ancestors did: because we *know* but do not *practice*. This is an unpleasant truth about common sense: it is not very common. We have reached the point where restatement of the obvious is the first duty of intelligent people.

The Book of Proverbs is a book of reminders. It is the voice of a wise, experienced parent, passing on to a willful child some basic truths that every generation past knew. This is one reason the book appeals to people of all ages. There is no "higher thought" in Proverbs, nothing vague or mystical. It is all about the day-to-dayness of life, about the small acts (and sometimes great acts) that turn into habits, good or bad. Those habits turn into what we call *character*. You might call Proverbs the Book of Character.

Some people say there is no theology in Proverbs. That is not so. God is there in the book, God the all-knowing, loving, merciful Father who wants his children to do right, for their own benefit, and for the benefit of the world at large. But theology is not the book's main concern. The emphasis is on *us*, human beings, inclined to be inconsiderate, vain, lacking in self-control, overly fond of the sound of our own voices. As children, we heard it frequently from adults: *Don't be selfish. Share what you have. Don't get mad. Don't pout. Don't follow the crowd in doing foolish, wicked things.* The Book of Proverbs exists because we did not pay enough attention to our parents, or to our Father. It is a book of authority, and what is authority but a means of using the knowledge of some for the benefit of others?

The book you are holding is intended to give you an intimate look at the Book of Proverbs—specifically, one hundred and one individual proverbs. When I say "intimate," I mean "up close and personal," for these wisdom-derived, God-given, authoritative words are never about someone else. They are about you, and for you, and for your good.

101 MOST POWERFUL PROVERBS IN THE BIBLE

1

Brain Stretching and Ear Tuning

The hearing ear and the seeing eye,
the LORD has made them both.

Proverbs 20:12

"ALL you have to do is pay attention." Thus said my scoutmaster back in Boy Scout days. Whatever we were learning—tying knots, flag signals—he firmly believed we could master it easily, so long as we paid attention to what he showed us. He told us that if we could memorize the lyrics to all the pop music hits (and we did), we could certainly learn to tie basic knots.

"All you have to do is pay attention." Thus said my college biology teacher. The class members were learning the life cycles of various forms of algae. It was neither fun nor exciting, yet he assured us the knowledge would have some value further down the line (not true), plus it "stretched the brain muscles" (so he said) to memorize the sequences of biological processes. He was right about the stretching. Our brain muscles got a good stretching, and memorizing was not so difficult, so long as we paid attention.

Another teacher sometimes used the phrase "He who has ears to hear, let him hear." I'm referring to Jesus, who often taught in parables, the simple stories with a deep meaning that not everyone grasped. Jesus knew what any teacher knows: the learner's alertness is a crucial part of the learning process. Even the best teacher cannot force-feed the lesson. God gives us our senses, God gives us teachers, but only we ourselves can supply the openness and willingness to learn.

Proverbs is a pay-attention book. Not faraway philosophers but sensible observers of the world wrote it. They had paid attention to life—their own lives, and those of others. They were passing on their life lessons to another generation. We are still learning those lessons today, as is evident by your reading this book. Most are so basic and simple—like two plus two. And, like two plus two, those moral lessons must be retaught to every generation.

It is in the nature of man that practically no one learns from experience. The mistakes of the fathers are lost on their children. Yet the fathers, if they are doing their duties, still try to pass on their experience-won wisdom to the children. If the children will use the eyes and ears God gave them, they do well. Every teacher and parent knows a child can "tune in" his eyes and ears to what truly interests him. The message of the Book of Proverbs is *Tune in to the greatest concern in human life: getting along well with others and being a person of integrity.*

If a group of hyperactive eleven-year-old Boy Scouts can memorize knots and a roomful of college students can memorize the life cycle of blue-green algae, surely people of faith can (if they use their eyes and ears) learn the basic lessons about a righteous life in this world.

Nothing that difficult. "All you have to do is pay attention."

Resolution: As you go through the rest of your day, stay alert to everything around you—as if you were going to be quizzed on your whole day.

2

No Walls, Bad City

*A man without self-control
is like a city broken into
and left without walls.*

Proverbs 25:28

K NOWLEDGE is power, but the best and most useful form of that power is power over ourselves." So said the philosopher Spinoza, whose words could have come straight from the Bible. As you may already know, the Bible is thoroughly pro-self-control, which puts it in opposition to our culture, which tells us that giving in to every selfish impulse is a good thing.

Our ancestors could not have grasped this. They would have asked the obvious questions: *How can you even develop a self if you have no self-control? How can people get along well in the world if each one is at the mercy of the others' impulses?*

Proverbs 25:28 compares self-control to the walls of a city. With no walls, a city was defenseless, almost certain to be attacked by enemies from without. With no self-control, a person is defenseless, certain to be at the mercy of his own impulses. Aside from his impulses harming himself, they can do tremendous damage to the people around him. Think of some basic problems of contemporary society—alcoholism, drug addiction, predatory sexuality, street crime—and you can trace them all to people giving in to their worst inclinations. And by failing to practice self-control, they grow less and less able to exert it. It is appropriate that Proverbs 25:28 uses the image of an undefended city: the main reason that so many cities today are hellish places to live is that so many of the inhabitants have no self-control. Graffiti, muggings, road rage, physical and verbal abuse, the taken-for-granted lack of courtesy that grates on everyone's nerves—chalk them all up to lack of self-control. Even when we aren't affected directly, we live in the fear of other people losing control.

One of my college classmates works with an after-school program with junior high kids, teaching them to abstain from sex until marriage. Does the program work? In terms of 100 percent effectiveness, no. In terms of some effectiveness, yes. Children and teens know something instinctively: you can't go through life without rules and boundaries. Some behaviors have to be off-limits. They expect adults to be boundary-setters, and they have more respect for the adult who says, "Just say no" than the adult who says, "When you do engage in sex, be sure to use protection, and . . ."

The same applies to drug and alcohol programs that emphasize "Just say no." It seems pretty clear that too many adults have abandoned their tasks as standard-setters and teachers of self-control, and the young folks have responded in the predictable way, not respecting those adults. Happily, some grown-ups prefer doing the right thing to being "cool," and kids respect this.

Kids need to hear the same message as adults: the real hero is the person who conquers his evil inclinations. Ultimately, the only power a person has is that which he exercises over himself. True power is knowing that you can, but you don't.

———

Resolution: Think of people you know who are severely lacking in self-control. Are those people happy? Have you ever considered suggesting to those people that they might try not giving in to all their impulses?

3

Sword Words

There is one whose rash words are like sword thrusts,
but the tongue of the wise brings healing.

Proverbs 12:18

ARE people all the same, anywhere on the globe? Yes—and no. One thing is constant. wherever there are humans, there is human nature. And part of human nature is unkindness. Since Cain and Abel, the story remains the monotonous same: humans harm each other. Cain chose the violent way, a way most of us call evil and strive to avoid. But there are many ways to do malicious mischief, and most of them are bloodless.

I attended a Christian college where there were few instances of actual physical violence among the students. That is the good news. The bad news is that a handful of students—both boys and girls— were absolutely ruthless in their use of words to do harm. They were highly skilled in the art of insults, attacking with tongues as sharp as daggers. In terms of speaking, they left no stone unhurled. It was part of the campus entertainment to say clever but cruel things, knowing that anyone listening would laugh—everyone but the person being insulted, that is. The target of the insults was, in fact, expected to shrug it off in public, to show they could take it.

This ability with words is an illustration of something true about humans, and particularly true about people who consider themselves Christians: people who would never resort to physical violence will gleefully do injury with their words. Laws are on the books to keep us from killing and maiming one another, and our whole culture at the present is ready to denounce anyone guilty of any form of physical abuse. Among people of faith, violence is not only illegal and socially disapproved but one better: something God detests. We know all this, and thus we avoid physical violence, or at least feel ashamed when we perpetrate it.

The Bible has much to say about bloodshed. It also has much to say about the tongue and its power for good and evil. More than once the Bible uses violent images to describe the power of the tongue: "The words of [the wicked man's] mouth were smoother than butter, but war was in his heart; his words were softer than oil, yet they were drawn swords" (Ps. 55:21 KJV). "The words of a talebearer are as wounds, and they go down into the innermost parts" (Prov. 18:8 KJV).

"War," "swords," "wounds"—sounds violent, yes? Yet our tolerance for hurting others with words is very high, and for the most obvious reason: we ourselves do harm with our words, and thus we don't take it seriously. But we do take words seriously when someone has harmed us. Considering that "do unto others as you would have them do unto you" is supposed to be our guide, we fail the divine test much too often. But it is so easy to sin with words, because they leave no fingerprints behind. And there is that great justifier of wrong: "Everyone does it."

Follow that up with: "True, but everyone *shouldn't*."

––––––––

Resolution: Utter no "sword words" today.

4

Taking Herself Lightly

A joyful heart is good medicine,
but a crushed spirit dries up the bones.

Proverbs 17:22

Years ago I lived next door to a young professional couple. Like the fictional nanny Mary Poppins, they were "practically perfect in every way"—so they believed. Both were young, slim, attractive, and well paid. I'll call them Eric and Kendra.

Kendra boasted that she ran five miles every day, which burnt a certain number of calories, which affected the metabolism, which affected the metabolizing of protein, and . . . Well, her knowledge of human physiology was most impressive. On the days when weather did not permit running, she had her treadmill. And she had a step machine. And dumbbells for the arms. And a very unpleasant routine for the abdominal muscles. And in her computer she kept a log of every change, no matter how minor.

She and Eric had no children. They were DINKs—double income, no kids. I could not imagine a child in their house anyway. It was too perfect. They had taken a creaky old home built in 1912 and turned it into a showplace: smoky-tinted windows, a kitchen that the Jetsons would have appreciated, wood floors so shiny they hurt the eyes. I never felt comfortable in it, however. Something in those achingly clean rooms, with every detail so carefully plotted and planned, made me feel I was in a temple, not a house. It was impressive, but it had no joy—nor did its owners.

But occasionally the temple had a noisy interruption—Kendra's sister Janice. She was pleasingly plump—to be truthful, downright fat. She and I clicked right away. Janice assured me that when she visited Eric and Kendra, she shopped for her own groceries. She wondered, as did I, why their diet did not turn them into rodents or rabbits or cattle. She asked that obvious question: why is it that people want to live past ninety if they spend their entire lives munching on food made for hoofed animals? And what about being strong and perfect? Wasn't that Hitler's goal, a world of physically flawless specimens?

Janice's laugh seemed to roll unencumbered right out of heaven. I think her whole body existed just to be a sounding board for laughter. Some say that width and wisdom go together. I don't know about that, but I do know that girth and mirth do. Janice was a woman stuffed with humor. She was a Christian of the best kind, that kind whose second greatest pleasure in life was laughter. (The first greatest pleasure was, I think, life itself, all of which she took as a gift from God.)

But I saw Janice cry, too. She cried—a lot—when Kendra learned she had MS, multiple sclerosis. She cried when Eric left Kendra. But she added a healthy dose of joy to Kendra's last years. Kendra, before she passed on, switched her loyalty from the god of Ego to the true God.

Janice, I am happy to report, is still living, still eating, still laughing. I have a feeling she will be laughing in heaven.

———

Resolution: Seek out a genuinely merry person, and find out what his or her secret is.

5

Honey-Speak

Gracious words are like a honeycomb,
sweetness to the soul and health to the body.

Proverbs 16:24

THE Bible literally drips with honey. It describes Israel, the home-land of God's people, time and time again as "a land flowing with milk and honey." Honey, something that occurred in nature (meaning it was a delightful gift from God), was one of the most pleasant things the ancient Hebrews knew. No wonder they applied the word to all sorts of pleasant things—including the Bible itself. Some Jewish schools still observe the old tradition of a student touching his lips to a page of the Torah with a drop of honey on it. To these students, the Word of God is delectable. (If only more Christians felt this way about the Bible!)

Most of us do not know enough people who are "honey-tongued." Recently I thumbed through my high school yearbooks and stopped to consider who the popular kids were. Most often they were the smart alecks, masters at the fine art of put-downs. You didn't get elected class president or homecoming queen by being sweet and kind. The typical popular kid went around acting as if he were life's only child, and thus had no need to say nice things. Belittling was the school sport.

And yet there were exceptions. It struck me that our student council president was an extremely likable guy—not only fun, but someone generous with compliments. Nothing dramatic, or showy, just mild pleasantries: "Nice shirt, Tim." "You did a good job in class, Susan." "Hey, nice car, Kevin." I don't recall the fellow ever putting anyone down. More importantly, he built people up.

A longtime friend of my parents died a few years ago. I visited the funeral home and was amazed at how many people were there. I hadn't known before how well liked the quiet, shy Mr. Burdett was. I kept overhearing, "He always had a kind word for everyone." I mentioned this later to his wife, who said, "Judd wouldn't let me gossip, even if it was just the two of us sitting by ourselves. He believed if you never said bad things, you would say only good things."

And so he lived. No one was ever sorry to see Judd arrive, or glad to see him go. His presence was as welcome as shade in summer or a fire at Christmas. He never tried to draw attention to himself. Yet when he died, people remembered him. The world is lessened by such people's passing.

In his classic novel *Vanity Fair*, William Makepeace Thackeray took a comical (and scornful) look at people's cruelty and manipulativeness. But in this lengthy book the author threw in a few characters that were actually worth admiring, such as Mr. Collingwood: "He never lost a chance of saying a kind word. Collingwood never saw a vacant place in his estate but he took an acorn out of his pocket and popped it in; so deal with your compliments through life. An acorn costs nothing, but it may sprout into a prodigious bit of timber."

Resolution: Compliment someone, and mean it.

6

Mighty Low

*Pride goes before destruction,
and a haughty spirit before a fall.*

Proverbs 16:18

ONE of the pleasures of traveling is looking at the colossal buildings our ancestors constructed. When I visited London for the first time, that famous old church, Westminster Abbey, caused my jaw to drop. The Gothic masterpiece is huge, of course, but it is even more impressive inside than out. England's kings have chosen to be married, crowned, and (in many cases) buried here. It is an appropriate resting place for the powerful.

I love such places, as most travelers do. Still, even as a tourist I carry faith in my head, and such impressive buildings make me pause to ask the obvious question: weren't these imposing structures built through oppressive taxation? Most of them were. And another question comes to mind: where are the kings and bishops now? All dead. Perhaps some of them are in heaven, but the others . . .

Back in your school days you might have read a famous poem, the sonnet "Ozymandias" by Percy Bysshe Shelley. The poem is about a colossal statue of a pharaoh in the Egyptian desert. The statue isn't in exactly mint condition—in fact, it has been broken in half. The traveler reads the inscription: "My name is Ozymandias, king of kings / Look on my works, ye mighty, and despair!" The poet has used irony here: the statue's inscription was originally intended to frighten other kings, who would tremble at the power of Ozymandias to commission such a huge statue of himself. But with the statue lying in the sand, the inscription has an altogether different meaning: *This is what becomes of earthly power, so, you mighty ones, consider that you yourselves will someday end up as I am.*

Interestingly, Shelley based his famous poem on a drawing he had seen of a real statue in the Egyptian sands. That statue, the archaeologists say, is of Rameses II, the oppressive pharaoh of the time of Moses and the Exodus. Consider: Moses is still praised as one of the great men in human history, while the once-mighty Rameses is practically forgotten, his stone image lying in pieces.

The message of "Ozymandias" could easily have been uttered by one of the Hebrew prophets, speaking out against the pride and pomp of the powerful empires of Egypt, Assyria, and Babylon. Throughout the Bible, and especially at the very end, in the Book of Revelation, we see the pattern: proud kings and proud nations fall. Where there were once capitals of empires, owls roost and hyenas howl. The colossal statues of ancient Egypt still impress the tourists, but the tourists do not fear the long-dead pharaohs. In their lifetimes the proud flew the pennants of their pride. Centuries later, camera-clickers admire the ruins.

Of course, most of us normal folk never have the opportunity to build or rule an empire. Our "kingdoms" are pretty much limited to our homes, our circle of friends, our fellow workers. But the warning about pride and destruction still applies. Each of us can narrow our vision, fascinated by our own looks, money, or cleverness. Proverbs 16:18 was not directed at the rulers of empires (who probably would not have heeded such advice anyway), but at us common folk, who too easily slip into pride and haughtiness.

———

Resolution: Think of proud people you have known personally, and ask yourself, Were they genuinely happy? *and* Did their happiness last?

7

Gray Knight

Gray hair is a crown of glory;
it is gained in a righteous life.

Proverbs 16:31

I HAVE known many gray-haired folk. My great-grandfather was one; everyone in the neighborhood called him "Uncle Levi." In the South, there is a certain type of male known as the "good ole boy," a type some people would approve of while others would not. But there is another type, approved by all: a "good man." Levi was such. He married one wife, for life, and never strayed. They pooled their virtues and pleased each other. Both belonged to the even-tempered order of humanity.

Levi never cursed. He never deceived anyone. In fact, I recall hearing more than a few people say, "Levi never lies," as if it was rare and remarkable, which it is. Levi never missed church on Sunday, even though I know he believed (as all good men do) that the Lord was with him the other six days of the week. Like all people of quiet virtue, he coped well with the disagreeables of ordinary life. He had manners, which made life serene for those around him. He appeared to be—and was—as simple as earth, as good as bread, as transparent as springwater.

One proverb Levi repeated was "An idle mind is the devil's workshop." It is one of those cliches with the virtue of being true. (Proverbs are short sentences based on long experience.) So Levi never "did nothing." He mowed, he raked, he pruned, he mended fences, he patched the roof, he even took time to answer my constant questions about what all of his tools in the shed did. And even when doing nothing, he did something—he whittled. The devil finds it hard to tempt men who whittle.

Cancer hit, and Levi slowed down—doing everything he did before, but less of it. He stayed indoors more, and I grew accustomed to seeing his big straw hat on the hook by the door most of the time, while in the past it was more often on his head, outdoors. My grandmother encouraged him to read, and he mumbled something like "Don't feel like readin'" and then read. He read the Bible, he read Westerns, he read whatever book I happened to be carrying around at the time. He had me read aloud, and it became a Saturday afternoon ritual, him on the bed, propped up on pillows and the headboard, me in the crook of his arm, reading to him.

One afternoon I fell asleep in that position. It had been a lazy autumn day, perfumed by fallen leaves, and we had both been drowsy as we read. I awoke feeling very chilly. I knew Levi must have been in a very deep sleep because he wasn't snoring anymore. I knew he kept his quilts in the closet, so I tried to raise up to get one, but I couldn't move. Levi's arm was tight and stiff around my neck. I touched his hand. It was like ice. I looked at his face—completely at peace.

I yelled for my grandmother, who came running from the kitchen, her hands wet and sudsy from dishwater. Within a second of entering the room she knew Levi was gone. I don't recall why I wasn't terrified at feeling that cold stiff arm around my neck.

Levi died "old and full of days," to borrow the Bible's phrase. He had worn a "crown of glory," to use the words of Proverbs 16:31. I am sure he is still wearing one.

Resolution: Seek the company of a godly senior citizen.

8

The Weight of Honesty

The LORD abhors dishonest scales,
but accurate weights are his delight.

Proverbs 11:1 (NIV)

I ASSUME that Christians are honest people—usually. That is, we generally avoid the more flagrant dishonesties of general society. We are slightly more inclined to tell the truth than the average person—or at any rate, we tell lies with a better motive. And you can trust us with money—at least large sums. But for people who preach that the degree of sin is less important than the *fact* of sin, we cut a pretty poor figure.

Honesty, after all, isn't so much a practice as an attitude of mind. It is one of the practical outworkings of the doctrine of loving our neighbors as ourselves. If you love your neighbor you won't cheat him; you would not want to be cheated yourself. If you love your neighbor you won't fail to repay a loan.

And you love your neighbor whether your neighbor is the man next door or the department supervisor. It is possible, even common, for a person to profess to follow Christ and to be dishonest in small things—taking felt-tip pens from the office, not telling the store clerk that she gave him a dollar extra in change, keeping a borrowed book until the person has forgotten he loaned it to him.

Practical honesty should be the easiest of all Christian practices, for it is quite basic. The Old Testament prophets knew all about the sort of person who offered large sacrifices to God on the Sabbath and shortchanged customers on weekdays. (Amos 8:5) There are Christians who talk glibly of spiritual growth and sanctification yet neglect to tell the waitress she made a mistake on the check.

Borrowing is a pregnant source of petty dishonesty. I wonder how many garages and closets are stocked with tools and appliances that originally were "borrowed." I've heard more than one story of someone going to a garage sale and finding his own possessions out on the table. It is no excuse to say there was no intention of stealing. There was indifference to another person's needs. There was carelessness with his property—which can't be called loving one's neighbors as oneself.

The days when most people worked either for themselves, for their families, or for some small company are long past. More and more people work for very large corporations, and the feeling seems to be that a corporation loses all claims on our honesty. A man who wouldn't dream of swiping a candy bar from the store thinks nothing of helping himself to office supplies. He has a dual scale of values—one for individuals, another for corporations. (Presumably the state and federal governments would qualify as large corporations also.) This isn't only muddled logic; it is blatant dishonesty.

The Book of Proverbs says nothing about swiping pens and paper from the office. It does say—more than once, in fact—that God "abhors dishonest scales," which means cheating in a business transaction. Most of us don't deal with literal "scales" in our work, but the principle applies: be honest at work, be honest everywhere.

Resolution: Consider ways that you are less than honest with your fellow workers or friends. Apologize, and make restitution.

9

Monumentally Immoral

Whoever walks in integrity walks securely,
but he who makes his ways crooked will be found out.

Proverbs 10:9

You don't have to be particularly religious to love a cathedral. They are some of the most beautiful buildings on the planet, and we have to credit the designers, masons, wood-carvers, and stained-glass-makers who created these amazing works. We also have to credit the people who contributed the enormous sums of money for such colossal projects.

Many of the people who contributed were saints—and many were not. In the Middle Ages—and today, for that matter—there were very unsaintly people who liked having their names associated with an impressive church. The stunning cathedrals scattered across Europe might not exist had it not been for people who were both immoral and wealthy, who expressed their vanity in funding and having their names emblazoned on grand churches. If investing in a church meant investing in eternity, heaven would be filled with very bad (but wealthy) people.

This is not all ancient history. America in the 1800s saw a wave of church construction. The day of the log frontier churches was passing, and rich merchants (who were supposedly Christian) contributed huge sums to build monuments to God (and themselves) in America's large cities. They also built church colleges and seminaries—and not surprisingly, some of these institutions were named for their benefactors.

One of these was Drew University, a Methodist school in New Jersey, named for Daniel Drew. If ever a Christian school bore the moniker of a vile character, this one does. Drew spent his life in pursuit of wealth, and he preferred the ill-gotten kind. In the early 1800s he was a cattle driver, one with the neat trick of mixing salt with the cattle's food, then driving them for days without water and at the journey's end, letting them drink their fill. The result? Full, fat-looking cattle he sold at a high price. (Essentially the buyer had bought leather skins filled with water.) Drew also "watered stock" by printing phony stock shares. He and some equally shady partners bilked Cornelius Vanderbilt out of millions.

But sometimes sharks eat other sharks. Drew's former partners tricked him out of part of his fortune. The supposedly Christian benefactor of Drew University died bankrupt. The school lives on, but Daniel Drew's fate is another matter entirely.

God moves in mysterious ways, and if unethical people are willing to build churches and schools that bring honor to him, so be it—even if their money was ill-gotten, and even if their motive was their own vanity, not the glory of the Lord.

————

Resolution: Ask yourself this question: if you had a huge sum of money to contribute to a church or religious school, would you be willing to do it anonymously?

Eagle Money

Do not wear yourself out to get rich;
have the wisdom to show restraint.
Cast but a glance at riches, and they are gone,
for they will surely sprout wings
and fly off to the sky like an eagle.

Proverbs 23:4–5 (NIV)

THE Book of Proverbs, like the Bible as a whole, has much to say about money. And why not? It is a basic human concern. With very few exceptions, people in the twenty-first century cannot live without it. No matter how "spiritual" we may be, we have to give some thought to the subject.

Proverbs 23:4–5 repeats a theme that wise men throughout the ages have known: wealth is never as stable as people think. Riches can, in the twinkling of an eye, "sprout wings / and fly off to the sky like an eagle." Everyone knows this, yet we can't help but be impressed by the sprawling homes of the rich. They *look* stable and permanent enough, and most poor and middle-class people would gladly trade places with the inhabitants. No wonder people line up to purchase lottery tickets, sometimes wasting their meager wages on the chance at quick riches.

The warning "Do not wear yourself out to get rich" isn't directed just at the rich themselves. It is directed at anyone—rich, poor, and in-between—who craves *more*. There are rich people who are satisfied with their lot, and poor who are satisfied with theirs. And there are people on every rung of the economic ladder who are most assuredly *not* satisfied with what they have. Human nature being what it is, those people will probably never be content, no matter how much they acquire. For such people, the words *enough* and *content* have no meaning at all.

Perhaps the apostle Paul had Proverbs 23:4–5 in mind when he wrote to his protege Timothy:

There is great gain in godliness with contentment, for we brought nothing into the world, and we cannot take anything out of the world. But if we have food and clothing, with these we will be content. But those who desire to be rich fall into temptation, into a snare, into many senseless and harmful desires that plunge people into ruin and destruction. (1 Timothy 6:6–9)

Paul followed with some of the most quoted (and *misquoted*) words of the Bible: "The love of money is a root of all kinds of evils" (v. 10).

Note the words: money is not evil, but *love of money* is. Any of us, from the poorest to the richest, can be motivated by that love. And any of us can be discontent. Why so, when the ideal state is "godliness with contentment"—something that is within everyone's grasp?

———

Resolution: Make a list of "absolute necessities" in life. Don't include wants but merely needs. Are you surprised to find what a short list it is? With some thought, you might even be able to make it shorter.

11

Adults and Adulterers

Why be captivated, my son, by an adulteress?
Why embrace the bosom of another man's wife?
For a man's ways are in full view of the LORD,
and he examines all his paths.

Proverbs 5:20–21 (NIV)

D ID you hear the joke about the traveling salesman? There are plenty of those jokes around, and they all involve sex. I have talked with enough salesmen to know the old stereotype is true: men on the road face a lot of sexual temptation.

"If you wanted to have a home and family *and* a wild and immoral life, my job would be ideal for it." Gene is a traveling sales representative, away from home about a third of the time. He admits that before he became a Christian his out-of-town trips always included stops at adult bookstores and strip clubs. He also admits that temptations still occur, and that his fellow salesmen take immorality in stride. "Our work can be pretty stressful. If we work hard, we prosper. If we don't, we bomb. And when you're in a strange town, a motel room can be lonely as a tomb. A sexual fling can seem like a release from your work and a cure for loneliness, too. It's easy to fall into this, because no one is watching you—except God."

"No one is watching—except God." Gene spoke of a case where a salesman was having an affair with a married woman whose husband was always away—with his job as a traveling salesman. The situation ended tragically for all four spouses. Two broken marriages, four unhappy spouses, and several unhappy children were involved. What might have happened if the parties remembered that their actions were, as Proverbs says, "in full view of the LORD"?

Gene explains that in his pre-Christian days his job was what it is for most people: making money to keep himself and his family at a certain standard of living. "It's a living, but not a life. Even after I became a Christian, I still looked at the job as just a way to put money in the bank. I was pleasing myself, my company, and the IRS, but I wasn't trying to please God.

"Then I met another sales rep, a mature Christian. He told me he'd had his own problems in the past with temptation on the road. He claimed that part of our problem is that our business contacts are pretty shallow, which is why we get lonely while traveling. He explained that spiritual intimacy with God is a better cure for loneliness than meaningless sexual intimacy."

Today, thanks to the Internet, a spouse does not have to have an on-the-road job to find adultery outlets. There are countless stories of husbands and wives who set up their extramarital flings while typing at a keyboard in the comfort of their own homes. But the Book of Proverbs is as up-to-date as the Internet, and its message still holds: he "examines all [our] paths."

———

Resolution: Talk to people you know who have happy marriages. How did they cope with times of separation?

12

Dedication Against the Grain

*One who is slack in his work
is brother to one who destroys.*

Proverbs 18:9 (NIV)

WORK has become a four-letter word for many people. Societies go through cycles—one generation works hard and plays little, another generation reverses the trend. Right now we seem to be in a pro-play, antiwork feeling. The "TGIF" mentality rules many workplaces, where employees see work as an annoying intrusion into the real purpose of life, hedonism.

"I enjoy the weekend as much as anybody," says Jennifer, a medical technologist at a large hospital. "But my fellow employees are the most leisure-obsessed people I've ever known. They're typical of the whole society. They live for Friday afternoons, and this fixation on getting free of work and heading for the beach means that Friday afternoons sometimes start *before* noon.

"Monday mornings are usually filled with people talking about what they did over the weekend," she continues. "Sometimes there's no serious work accomplished before lunch break." The pattern reverses itself at the end of the week. "On Fridays most of my coworkers might as well not show up. Lots of them duck out before their official quitting time, and even when they're here they're discussing their plans for the weekend."

Jennifer's comments echo estimates by some corporate observers who believe that a forty-hour workweek actually consists of about twenty hours—after you subtract the time spent in late starts, early quits, overly long breaks and lunch hours, foot-dragging, and just plain idling. "They pay me for forty hours. I try to give them that," Jennifer says, "even though I get some flack from other employees about being a workaholic. I'm definitely not that. But when I see our employees using computers to play games during work time, it angers me. I've seen patients show up waiting to have a test done, and the person who is supposed to wait on them is playing poker on the computer."

As Jennifer observed, it is a sin and a crime to work twenty hours and get paid for forty. It cheats the employer, and it is unfair to clients who should expect better service. Spiritually speaking, it dishonors God, for it suggests that our work has no real value beyond the paycheck.

Are there rewards for honesty and hard work? "Oh, I've gotten an Employee of the Month citation more than once. That counts for something, but more important to me is that I see my job as an area where I'm not pressed into the world's mold. I wrote out a Bible verse on conformity and taped it in my locker at work." Jennifer was referring to Romans 12:2 (NIV): "Do not conform any longer to the pattern of this world, but be transformed by the renewing of your mind. Then you will be able to test and approve what God's will is— his good, pleasing and perfect will." Jennifer adds, "It isn't just me and God. In a hospital with this many employees, Christians find each other. Friday morning at 6:45 we have a brief gathering in the cafeteria. One thing we always pray for is that our attitudes won't be affected by other employees'. On the day of the week that takes the prize for laziness, that's pretty important."

———

Resolution: Talk to Christians who work hard at their jobs. What is their attitude toward coming in late, leaving early, taking long breaks? Are they criticized for not following the world's standards?

13

More Awesome Than Pizza

The fear of the LORD is the beginning of knowledge;
fools despise wisdom and instruction.

Proverbs 1:7

"OUR pizzas are awesome!" So said the young woman at my local supermarket. She was referring to the ones made in the store deli. I wondered what she would do if I walked to the deli counter and fell down trembling in front of the pizzas there. Wouldn't that be the right response if their pizzas were "awesome"? I did try their pizza. It was "tasty," "good," or maybe even "*real* good." But not "awesome."

I learned in a college history class that the Russian ruler Ivan the Terrible got his famous nickname because he was "awesome," for in the old days *terrible* meant something like *awe-inspiring* or even *terrifying*. He was Ivan the Awesome—meaning a powerful person you respected, obeyed, and left alone. (Since Ivan really was a thoroughly nasty character, it is appropriate that as *terrible* changed meaning, the name still stuck to him.)

The Bible presents us with a truly awesome God—the Creator and Sustainer of everything, the All-Knowing and All-Powerful. He is loving and merciful and forgiving, yes—and approachable. But he deserves, and demands, respect. And this is why you see the phrase "fear of the Lord" so often in the Old Testament. Past generations of human beings understood this: of course you *feared* God, for God was *awesome*. And (unlike Ivan) God is holy and perfect, while humans are sinful and flawed, meaning we are not God's equals.

The Book of Proverbs is a book of wisdom, a practical guide to living intelligently and morally in the world. Obviously no one can do this without the right foundation, and according to Proverbs 1:7, that foundation is "the fear of the Lord." The God of Proverbs, and of the whole Bible, is God who must be obeyed. Do so, and live well. Defy him, and live badly.

The Bible has a name for people who cannot accept the awesome God: *fools*. Doesn't that name apply perfectly to anyone who cannot accept the basic reality that God is in charge and wants his creatures to treat each other with compassion and fairness? This word appears many times in Proverbs, and it never refers to mental deficiency but to moral weakness.

As we read through some of the best proverbs, keep 1:7 in mind: wisdom and right behavior are rooted in the wise and perfect God. Lose sight of him, and life goes seriously wrong.

Pizza isn't even in the same category.

———

Resolution: Think back to authority figures in your life whom you respected and perhaps feared—parents, teachers, coaches, supervisors. Were there some who almost intimidated you? How did that affect your desire to please them?

14

Outloving the Pagans

Whoever despises his neighbor is a sinner,
but blessed is he who is generous to the poor.

Proverbs 14:21

T HE Spirit of the Lord is on me, / because he has anointed me /
to preach good news to the poor"—so said Jesus (Luke 4:18
NIV), and the Old and New Testaments support his advocacy for the
poor. (See, for just a few examples, 1 Samuel 2:7–8, Psalms 34:6,
69:35, 72:12–13, 102:17, 107:9, Isaiah 41:17, Luke 1:46–53, James
2:5.) The Bible's message is clear: if you are a person of faith, you
care for the indigent. *Care* means more than striking an attitude. It
means actively working to benefit destitute individuals.

In terms of compassion, how did the early Christians compare
with the surrounding pagan culture? Quite well. Christians impressed even their critics. "Behold, how these Christians love one another!" said one noted unbeliever, the pagan critic Celsus. Christians
introduced a new idea into the Roman world: caring for the frail, the
unprotected. The pagans worshiped power and sneered at weakness.
If the poor fell by the wayside, well, that was their fate.

The earliest Christians, with no church buildings or professional clergy to maintain, could give all their gifts to the poor. Many Christians willed their estates "to Christ" or "to the poor," and the nearest church (a group of believers, not a building) would distribute the funds to the needy nearby. Gifts took various forms: food, clothing, buying back people sold into slavery, releasing people from debtors' prisons, visiting prisoners persecuted for their faith. In an age when a poor person could hardly expect a decent burial, Christians gave much attention to proper burial for fellow believers.

Emperor Constantine ended persecution and made Christianity legal in 313. Being legal, it eventually became respectable. With no personal risk in being a believer, anyone could become one. The halfhearted Christian became a fixture. The halfhearted are not generous givers.

Something new arose: church buildings, which with time became larger and more opulent. Giving money "to the church" could mean aiding the poor—or adding stained glass. Many rich folk chose to memorialize their generosity in stone rather than in flesh.

As church buildings grew, so did the prestige of the clergy, particularly bishops. Some clergymen were shining lights of compassion. At times bishops sold their costly robes and communion ware to aid the poor in famines. But many clergy became rich through money that should have aided the poor.

Yet the church's care for the poor never ceased. Pope Gregory the Great (c. 600) supervised free bread-and-soup lines in Rome and organized "runners" who carried hot food to shut-ins. In an age of few inns, churches provided inexpensive shelter for travelers. During plagues, when people deserted the cities in droves, many Christians stayed on to comfort the dying poor and give them a proper burial.

Jesus predicted that his followers would work miracles—and that they would minister to the poor. The miracles and ministries still continue. People of faith still bless the poor with their generosity, and as Proverbs 14:21 says, they themselves are blessed.

Resolution: Make some phone calls or talk to friends about getting involved in some ministry to the poor in your area.

15

The Anxious Bench

Anxiety in a man's heart weighs him down,
but a good word makes him glad.

Proverbs 12:25

Since this world is not our final destination, it shouldn't surprise us that it is not a secure place. No situation is certain, and no job is guaranteed to last us a lifetime. I discussed this with Leanne, a midlevel manager at a utility company. She is well paid, and her job befits her background and training. Even so, for more than a year Leanne and her coworkers suffered from anxiety over whether their jobs would last much longer.

"You'd think a utility company is the ultimate security," she said. "After all, people always need electricity, right? But a rumor leaked out from headquarters that several midlevel positions were being phased out. For over a year I walked around knowing I could be axed at any time. Every time a memo appeared on the bulletin board, people flocked around, looking desperate. It was easy for me to get caught up in the fear, the feeling of *Oh, no, what will become of me?* I was surrounded by people who were filled with resentment that any day their lives could be changed dramatically."

Millions of people share that predicament. Downsizings occur even in booming firms. Is it possible to "work for the Lord" when we have so little security? "Definitely," Leanne says. "In fact, I think that painful year when I lived with the threat of downsizing gave me a new perspective on my job. I love it, and truth to tell, I was on the verge of worshiping it. That's wrong—it's idolatry to worship anything except God. So I started every day by praying during my morning commute, 'Help me remember, Lord, that my only real security is you.'"

Did the downsizing occur? "It did, and, thankfully, my job was spared. But my attitude has stayed the same: I have a life, whether or not I'm holding this particular job."

I asked Leanne how she reacted to the layoff of her coworkers. "Almost everyone who was laid off went to a local bar after work that day. I don't drink, but I went with them, had a soda, just sat and listened while they alternated between whining and trying to cheer themselves up. I truly felt for them.

"I kept quiet until someone finally said, 'Okay, Leanne, since you lucked out and kept your job, what are you doing here with us losers?' I told them that they weren't losers unless their whole lives consisted of just their jobs. I told them I'd pray for them all—that provoked a few cynical smiles, but I think most people appreciated my being there." Leanne went a step further than praying: she helped her church start a support group for people who are unemployed. In short, during a stressful time for a large group of people, Leanne managed not to be weighed down by anxiety. The good words of assurance from the Scriptures made her glad, as Proverbs 12:25 says, and she in turn helped to lighten the load of her fellow workers.

———

Resolution: Start each morning with a prayer to God to keep you free from worry and anxiety. Make it a point each day to say a cheerful word to some anxious person.

16

Tea Equality

Rich and poor have this in common:
The LORD is the Maker of them all.

Proverbs 22:2 (NIV)

"ADAM's ale" is an old phrase meaning *water*—the idea being that man's original thirst-quencher was the most basic drink of all, pure water. But God gave us a more varied menu than that, and milk from various sources was always around, and the juices of whatever fruits were squeezable. God gave us thirst, and a multitude of quenchers.

Then, of course, for the southerner, there is tea—iced, that is. Iced tea is perhaps the finest thing ever poured down a human throat. Anyone who ever lived through a Deep South summer would agree.

Like all great things, iced tea is simple: some dry black leaves, sugar (more about that in a moment), lemon (optional, but not really), and water. And it must be good water, not some thousand-time-filtered something in a plastic bottle. My granddad was of the opinion that our local water, with a serious amount of limestone flavoring it, was the best in the world, and I have found no reason to disagree. Boil the good limey water, toss in the tea, let it steep a few minutes, then thank God.

There are disagreements on the amount of sugar in iced tea. My aunt likes hers *very* sweet—so much so that if you set a pitcher of it on the windowsill, hummingbirds would flock to it. My mother was less prodigal with the sugar, but not much. I use a little less myself, and it is perfect, in my own tongue's opinion. At family gatherings, there are several pitchers around at any moment, each with a different amount of sugar added.

This has been the Great Southern Exercise in Democracy: the glass of iced tea, wonderful at any time, but most of all on a sweltering summer afternoon, so humid that the glass (real glass, and usually clear) always sweated in your hand. No one ever analyzed it, but we knew that just as the heat and humidity were roasting all of us, rich and poor, high and low, so we were all coping with it in the same way—a fan, a rocking chair, a glass of the Great Leveler, iced tea. Sun on the evil and the good, rain on the just and the unjust, tea for the saint and the sinner and all those in between. The fancy folks on the hill sweltered and drank their iced tea, as did the dirt farmer, the teacher, the preacher, the mechanic, the banker, the trucker. Heat, humidity, sweat for everyone, all who toil at the Great Grindstone, earth—and the one solution, tea, for everyone.

"The Lord is maker of them all"—rich and poor and in-between, sending them such blessings as sun and rain and tender green leaves and flowers every spring, and golden autumn afternoons, and a thousand other simple pleasures that rich and poor can take for granted, or praise God for.

———

Resolution: Think of the many blessings God gives that are shared by both rich and poor.

17

No Useless Saints

Whoever works his land will have plenty of bread,
but he who follows worthless pursuits lacks sense.

Proverbs 12:11

M y mother had a favorite expression: "Make yourself useful."
I never questioned the meaning of that word "useful,"
since I assumed it meant helping her or my father with the work
around the house, lawn, or garden. I knew that certain activities
were *not* useful: watching television, reading, playing songs on my
record player, or coloring with crayons. At times I was overjoyed
when I could engage in one of these useless pursuits, though often I
felt a twinge of guilt. I felt even more guilty if I was actually doing
nothing. Much as I enjoyed playing make-believe games in my mind,
I took great pains to at least *appear* busy most of the time.

Later my parents' attitude changed slightly, and I learned that
buying records and toys was good (thus presumably useful) because
it showed that they had been industrious enough to provide me with
those things.

It is true that the past is always present, and we never fully outgrow our childhoods. I have not lived at home for many years, but I

still become anxious when I am not being "useful." (This is one reason I write—I fear that my thoughts go to waste unless I commit them to paper.) I haven't learned to appreciate much the joys of extended laziness. Even now I'm wondering what I can accomplish during an upcoming week's vacation at an isolated cottage on Lake Michigan. (After all, *something* must come out of that week.)

I think back to my grandfather, a cotton farmer. Spring, summer, and fall, he was busy—and generally happy. In winter he grew bored and crabby. Somehow books and television did not seem as rewarding to him as work, even if he did complain about sweating under a hot southern sun.

Cultures experience various swings of the pendulum. My grandfather's generation honored people who worked hard. My generation honors people who play hard—or more accurately, who have money to spend on leisure. Perhaps there is a happy medium somewhere in there, but I think my grandfather—and Proverbs—was more on the right track. Hard work never killed anyone. But laziness and leisure (too much of them, anyway) have led to debt, bankruptcy, frustration, and bitterness. Perhaps a generation that comes after mine will learn this lesson, probably from the mistakes of their own parents. "Work" is not, in the Bible's view, a "four-letter word," and neither is "hard." Our present generation needs to remember the advice of Proverbs, and think more highly of work and a little less lovingly of leisure and laziness.

———

Resolution: Talk to some older people who worked hard in their lives. Were they satisfied when they worked? Did they enjoy their work more than they enjoy their retirement now?

18

Wordless About Words

When words are many, transgression is not lacking,
but whoever restrains his lips is prudent.

Proverbs 10:19

F OR years I kept a diary, in which I included the topic of every Sunday sermon I heard. A notable omission: I never heard a pastor preach on the power of the tongue. This doesn't mean that pastors *never* speak on the subject, just that it is, to state the obvious, a neglected topic. Why so, since the Bible says so much about it? Why so, since great Christian thinkers through the ages have had much to say as well?

My own theory: I think pastors overlook it because it seems "small"—so petty that their congregations might think them nitpicky if they preach on it. My other theory: it makes people uncomfortable. Most of us are, whether we admit it or not, guilty of verbal sins.

I think spoken offenses are Christians' pet sins, since we don't consider them all that important, and since gossip and rumoring are habits we don't wish to break. Consider the story of David and his wife Michal, found in 2 Samuel 6:16–23. David, king of Israel and a very emotional sort, literally danced in the streets of Jerusalem to celebrate the bringing of the ark of the covenant into the city. Instead of praising his public enthusiasm, Michal greeted him with a sneering rebuke: you've made a spectacle of yourself today, dancing in the streets like a commoner! I suspect that most wives (and probably quite a few husbands, too) read this story and secretly sympathize with the waspish Michal.

Yet there will be, ultimately, a final reckoning for us all: "People will give account for every careless word they speak, for by your words you will be justified, and by your words you will be condemned" (Matt. 12:36–37).

The Book of Proverbs—and the whole Bible, actually—is clear: God takes our words seriously. And so should we. Our mouths are lethal weapons, yet there is no "tongue control" movement comparable to gun control. Thus we do much harm—to those we injure with our words, and to ourselves because we are so much less than God intends us to be. I fear this is a form of hypocrisy that we shrug off too easily, something the apostles sternly warned against: "If anyone thinks he is religious and does not bridle his tongue but deceives his heart, this person's religion is worthless" (James 1.26).

"Restrain[ing] the lips" is a nice phrase from Proverbs 10. What if there was a cultural movement to do this? It would produce far more good in the world than the current one to restrain the appetite for food, wouldn't it? People may indeed hurt themselves by taking in too much fat and cholesterol. But the wounds from words are far worse.

Worth remembering: there is always time to add a word, but none in which to take one back. Also worth remembering: "Whoever restrains his lips is prudent."

———

Resolution: Put yourself on a "word diet" for at least a day. Pledge yourself to say nothing mean or cruel, but only something kind or constructive.

19

Leftover Righteousness

When the tempest passes, the wicked is no more,
but the righteous is established forever.

Proverbs 10:25

WHEN was the last time you heard someone referred to as "righteous"? Probably a long time ago—or never. The word, so common in the Bible, has fallen on evil times. In the age of Political Correctness, the average person isn't really aware of the difference between *righteous* and *self-righteous*. In the Bible, of course, the difference is huge: righteousness is good, but self-righteousness (rooted in pride) is bad.

But to many people today, *righteous* has come to mean *pompous*, *judgmental*, and *intolerant*—all of which are bad. Most people, including many Christians, would cringe if someone referred to them as "righteous." A person would take pleasure in being called "a nice guy," "cool," or "a lot of fun." But "righteous"? Brrr.

Still, the Bible is absolutely saturated with the concept of righteousness. And why not? God himself is fully righteous, and he expects humans to be. What does the word actually mean? The Hebrew word we translate as "righteous" meant "just." A righteous person is fair and honest in his dealings, showing no partiality to the powerful, but showing compassion to the oppressed. If a righteous person is "intolerant," he is intolerant of dishonesty and exploitation. A righteous person hates not people, but injustice and abuse.

In other words, the Bible's concept of righteousness should appeal to most people—even to the Politically Correct. Perhaps it is unfortunate that Bible translators can't find a valid word to substitute for "righteous." But in the meantime, we can hope that pastors (and authors) explain to believers what the rich meaning of the word is.

The Book of Proverbs focuses on being both wise and righteous. Obviously the two go together—a man is more righteous the more wisdom he has (or to be precise, the more wisdom he *uses*). The goal of becoming righteous is clearly to please God—and to live well, even if the righteous are not always rewarded in this life. Proverbs 10:25 states that the righteous person is established "forever," while the wicked pass away. This is one of the great comforting messages of the Bible: whatever is good never ends. The righteous God is eternal, and righteous souls share in eternity. Wickedness is, in a sense, *trash*—useless and discarded. It does not belong in the universe of good things God created. Righteousness does, which is why it endures forever.

If someone calls you "righteous," take it as a compliment.

Resolution: Think of people you know who would fit the Bible's definition of "righteous." Do you think these people would be pleased to be called righteous? Why or why not?

20

Pennies and Purple

A kindhearted woman gains respect,
but ruthless men gain only wealth.

Proverbs 11:16 (NIV)

W E do not know her name, but pastors have probably preached more sermons about her than any other woman in the Bible. I'm referring to the nameless widow whose story two of the Gospels tell:

> And he [Jesus] sat down opposite the treasury and watched the people putting money into the offering box. Many rich people put in large sums. And a poor widow came and put in two small copper coins, which make a penny. And he called his disciples to him and said to them, "Truly, I say to you, this poor widow has put in more than all those who are contributing to the offering box. For they all contributed out of their abundance, but she out of her poverty has put in everything she had, all she had to live on." (Mark 12:41–44)

Jesus had good reason to appreciate generous women. The Gospels tell us that Mary Magdalene and several other women provided for Jesus and the disciples "out of their means." Just how much financial support they gave we are not told, nor would the amount matter. It is clear Jesus gratefully accepted their support, just as he was pleased with the woman who anointed his feet with a container of expensive perfume (John 12).

Likewise the apostles had reason to praise compassionate women. Paul commended his friend Priscilla, as well as Chloe and Nympha—all three of whom hosted Christian fellowships in their homes. (See 1 Cor. 1:11, 16:19, and Col. 4:15.) And of course there was the famous Lydia, whom the author of Acts called a "dealer in purple cloth" (16:14), a successful businesswoman who was Paul's first Christian convert in Europe, and who later gave support to a new fellowship. John addressed his second epistle to "the elect lady and her children" (v. 1)—which might (so the scholars say) refer to a church and its members, but possibly refers to a Christian woman and her actual children.

The Bible says very little about how women *looked*. We are told that villainous Queen Jezebel "painted her eyes [and] arranged her hair" (2 Kings 9:30). But we never learn how the *good* women looked. The giving heart is more important than the appearance—and come to think of it, that is true for men as well as women.

Bad or "ruthless" men—as Proverbs 11:16 (NIV) refers to them—are condemned, regardless of what they look like. They "gain only wealth"—meaning that they acquire with no desire to share the blessing with others. The Bible praises kindhearted women. Anyone who says the Bible is "sexist" or "antiwoman" clearly has never read the passages that commend these generous, loving, compassionate people.

Resolution: Thumb through the Gospels and Acts and pay attention to the various women. Also, note that at the end of each of Paul's letters he addresses certain specific individuals, including some notable Christian women.

21

Reserved for Good

*Death and life are in the power of the tongue,
and those who love it will eat its fruits.*

Proverbs 18:21

SEVERAL years ago I published a book of presidential trivia. During radio interviews to promote the book, I was often asked, "Which was your favorite president?" I had to admit I was intrigued by Calvin Coolidge, "Silent Cal," a president who definitely took Proverbs 18:21 to heart.

While many recent presidents have obviously delighted in the sounds of their own voices, Silent Cal kept his verbiage to a minimum. Our world values people who are gabby, and many people interpreted Coolidge's reticence as a sign of stupidity. This wasn't so. The Vermont-born Coolidge was a highly intelligent man, one who, for his own pleasure, translated Dante's *Divine Comedy* from Italian into English. He also wrote poetry, though hardly anyone knew about it. He was one of the last presidents to compose most of his own speeches, which were well written—and brief. He was both smart and opinionated, but felt no compulsion to constantly flaunt his intelligence or air his opinions.

In his *Autobiography*, Coolidge wrote of "the value of a silence which avoids creating a situation where one would otherwise not exist . . . the bad taste and the danger of arousing animosities and advertising an opponent by making an attack on him." "I have always had more of an ambition to *do* things than merely to talk about doing them." "You don't have to explain something you never said." "I don't recall any candidate for president that ever injured himself very much by not talking." "Perhaps one of the reasons I have been a target of so little abuse is because I have tried to refrain from abusing other people."

In his biography of Coolidge, *A Puritan in Babylon*, journalist William Allen White noted "that his emotions were hidden did not lessen their power." "Because Coolidge knew human nature well, he dared not talk casually to the men he met officially." Was Silent Cal a great president? Perhaps not. He had the good fortune to preside when the country was relatively prosperous, so he had to contend with no wars or major disasters. We have no idea how he would have fared during a war—or the Depression that followed a few months after he left office.

Yet he was a very *good* president, or rather a very good man—a loyal husband and father, an affectionate son who even as an adult kissed his father in public, a man of total integrity (a "Puritan in Babylon," as his biographer called him), a man whose politics were rooted in common sense and basic Christian morals.

Coolidge's understanding of "the value of a silence" is remarkable in a public figure. He never lied nor made grand promises. If he was not a world-changing and heroic president, he was certainly the kind of wise and righteous soul Proverbs speaks of, a man with a clear understanding of the power of the tongue. We can only speculate about what the world would be like if statesmen today understood that "death and life are in the power of the tongue." With their own souls anchored in God and his love, they can, as the Proverb says, "defend the rights of the poor and needy."

———

Resolution: Think of people you know who are quiet and reserved. Are they, on the whole, good people? Do you think their reticence is due to shyness, lack of intelligence, or something else?

22

Very, Very Worldly Workers

A generous man will himself be blessed,
for he shares his food with the poor.

Proverbs 22:9 (NIV)

CHRISTIANS have been accused of being "otherworldly" people. It's true. From the very beginning, they have had heaven on their minds. But it is a curious phenomenon: people who are otherworldly seem to do so much good in this world. They are so conscious of the Lord's generosity that they are generous themselves—people who bless others and are blessed themselves, as Proverbs 22:9 has it.

In the 1800s many countries became increasingly industrialized. People left the farms and began working in mines and factories, often for low wages and in abominable working conditions. The wealthy English evangelicals known as the Clapham Sect chose to attack the problems with legislation. Having social and political clout, they worked to pass parliamentary laws that restricted working hours for women and children and enforced safety and health standards. The Clapham Sect introduced a new element in Christian concern for the poor: passing humane laws.

One of the Clapham leaders, William Wilberforce, wrote *A Practical View of the Prevailing Religious System of Professed Christians in the Higher and Middle Classes, Contrasted with Real Christianity.* The book is usually just called *Real Christianity*, but the whole title is worth noting. Wilberforce claimed that the only remedy for the selfishness that wealth encouraged was to turn from nominal belief to the active Christianity of personal commitment. The book was a phenomenal best-seller.

Humane laws could not solve all the problems, of course. Victorian England with its grimy city slums needed "foot soldiers" for the Lord. These came in the form of William Booth and his Salvation Army. In the 1860s, when Booth looked at industrial London he saw overcrowded homes, drunkenness, domestic violence, prostitution, and unemployment. He believed if people knew Christ, their behavior— and conditions—would change.

Booth didn't ignore physical needs. He set up Food for the Million shops, offering cheap meals. In severely cold winters the Salvation Army sold coal at rock-bottom prices. In sizzling summers they sold "penny ice." The army ran "working girls' homes" so that women on low wages could live in a clean, safe place. They also organized "woodyards," where able-bodied men could chop firewood to earn their keep.

Booth warned against "indiscriminate charity" and "coddling" for the lazy. He respected the poor enough to believe they wanted the dignity of helping themselves, of paying at least a nominal amount for what they received. He had no time for lazy freeloaders. He was wise enough to see that there are people who, the more you do for them, the less they will do for themselves.

Some "establishment" Christians scoffed at the army's bands and uniforms. But even scoffers observed that under the army's influence, prostitution, drunkenness, and family violence decreased in the cities. Homelessness and hunger lessened. One cynical member of Parliament remarked, "These buffoons will in time make the slums resemble Her Majesty's palace." That didn't happen, but thousands of urban poor improved themselves—spiritually and materially—thanks to faithful believers like the Salvation Army folk.

———

Resolution: Offer a special prayer for people who minister face to face with the poor.

23

Lying Down with the Dogs

He who walks with the wise becomes wise,
but the companion of fools will suffer harm.

Proverbs 13:20

L ет's begin by remembering that in the Bible the word "fool"
doesn't mean merely *stupid person* but also *moral degenerate.* So
we could paraphrase Proverbs 13:20 as "You do well to hang around
with only the wise and moral people." This isn't the only warning in
the Bible against hobnobbing with bad folk. The Old Testament, especially the Psalms, encourage us to avoid soiling ourselves by keeping company with the wicked.

Sounds intolerant, doesn't it? And intolerance is not tolerated
today. In the modern view of things, avoiding corrupt people would
be "judgmental"—as if any of us had any right to call someone else
"bad"! But the Bible has no such qualms. We should, so it tells us,
avoid thieves, murderers, gluttons, boozers—and also gossips, slan-
derers, and dishonest businessmen.

And yet . . . didn't Jesus himself sit down at the table with despised people such as prostitutes and tax collectors? He did indeed.
He reached out to them and loved them. And he made converts. But

most of us aren't equipped to do that. Hanging around bad people presents good people with temptations—notably the temptation to condone their depraved behavior. In our age of "tolerance," this temptation is very strong. Jesus had the rare ability to mingle with sinners without winking at their behavior. I can't do that, and I don't know many people who can. Perhaps Jesus knew the delicate art of making a point without sounding preachy.

I recall my great-grandfather referring to a local man whom no one would speak to because the man was a notorious wife-beater. Decades ago, this was not uncommon—ostracizing a cruel person. In certain country clubs, a man who abused his wife or kept a mistress might be voted out of the club. During the Civil War, southerners would cross the street to avoid passing by "speculators"—the greedy exploiters who hoarded supplies and hiked up the prices. Sometimes they cursed these men or pelted them with mud. This had an effect: such people knew that decent people condemned their behavior. The decent people believed that cordiality to a known rascal would be interpreted as condoning his deeds.

Today, on the other hand, is there any way of letting people know their behavior is wrong? Not really. More likely today's society would condemn the "judgmental" person more heartily than the rogue. Yet the Word of God stands firm, as we see in this proverb: making companions of bad folks can corrupt one's own morals, and can lead the wicked to believe their bad behavior is not important. And how can people of faith be "the light of the world" and "salt of the earth" if we smile and condone what is plainly evil?

Resolution: Think of times you have held back your opinions for fear of being called "judgmental" or "intolerant." Think of times you engaged in some activity you believed was wrong but didn't want to be criticized by your friends.

24

The Lions Club

The wicked flee when no one pursues,
but the righteous are bold as a lion.

Proverbs 28:1

THOUGH I never served in the military, I admit to being utterly fascinated by a soldier named Thomas J. Jackson, better known to history as "Stonewall." The amazing Jackson was a fierce fighter and strategist—and as a devout Christian who prayed almost constantly, who taught a Sunday school class for slaves, and who tried, whenever possible, to avoid fighting on Sundays.

The shy, quiet Confederate general was utterly lacking in vanity. Yet he was amazingly bold, and as one of his biographers put it, "He feared neither man nor devil, but he feared God." His destiny was, he believed, in the hands of God, so he performed his military duties without anxiety. The South grieved deeply when Jackson died from wounds inflicted by friendly fire. Jackson himself accepted his fate: "It is God's will." He had lived as one of those very rare individuals who take the Bible as a guide to conduct.

Jackson was a Presbyterian and an admirer of the founder of Presbyterianism, the Scottish reformer John Knox. The brassy Knox had no qualms about confronting his country's ruler, the famous Mary, Queen of Scots. Certain he was doing the will of the Lord, Knox went about the business of reforming the Scottish church and was not about to let a wayward queen or rowdy noblemen stand in his way. When Knox died in 1572, a speaker at his funeral stated that Knox "neither feared nor flattered any flesh." He was righteous and as Proverbs 28:1 has it, "bold as a lion."

Most of us think of Christians as being "nice" people. Rightly so. Both Jackson and Knox were incredibly warm and loving men—usually. But some occasions call for courageous action. Readers of the Gospels know that Jesus himself was not always "nice" in the usual sense. All four Gospels record the story of Jesus in the temple courts, driving out the money changers with a whip. They had, as Jesus said, turned a house of prayer into "a den of thieves" (Matt. 21:13 KJV), and this called for a whip and audacity. It isn't most people's favorite image of Jesus, but you can't deny it is part of the Bible's record.

Martin Luther, a bold character himself, wrote that "the pagan trembles at the rustling of a leaf." He was echoing Proverbs 28:1: the wicked and unbelievers inhabit a frightening, threatening universe, yet the Christian has nothing to fear, for ultimately his fate is in God's hands.

Living the kind of life God intended requires different kinds of courage. We need a quiet kind to say no to temptations, to exercise self-control in a world that constantly shouts, "Indulge yourself!" At other times, we may need to face the foe with the lionheartedness that Jackson, Knox, and Jesus himself exhibited. The wicked face the world with no assurance that anyone is on their side, while the righteous have the greatest ally of all, God himself.

Resolution: Think of people you have known who were genuinely bold and courageous. Were they people of faith?

25

Rescue the Perishing

Rescue those who are being taken away to death;
hold back those who are stumbling to the slaughter.

Proverbs 24:11

MOST people are aware that many early believers died in the sporadic persecutions throughout the Roman Empire. Persecution did not always mean death, however, but deprivation. When the emperors were engaging in anti-Christian campaigns, they often sentenced persons accused of following the suspicious religion to work in mines, or they might confiscate all their worldly goods. For some families this was more traumatic than martyrdom of one of the members. But the fellowships were quick to come to the aid of these "living martyrs" and their families.

In the year 303 the fiercest persecution took place under Emperor Diocletian, who insisted that the Christians sacrifice to the pagan gods. Death and torture occurred everywhere, and the emperor destroyed or appropriated both individuals' and entire churches' property. But the survivors did not languish in their new poverty, for the ones who retained the most property helped those who lost everything. The Christians' display of love to persecuted brethren dealt another blow to paganism, in spite of Diocletian's attempts to revive it.

Abortion was widespread in the Roman Empire. Most citizens saw no moral problem in disposing of the unwanted unborn child. But early Christian writings show that the faithful would not do this. The believers of those days applied the Bible's concern for the weak and oppressed to the weakest members of society, the unborn.

The Romans had no qualms about killing the newly born. Among the pagans, obvious birth defects signalled exposing the child to the elements—wolves, vultures, or inclement weather. The Romans had clearly inherited the Greeks' obsession with physical perfection. As a child grew, some other defects—mental retardation, for example—might manifest themselves. Few pagan families would tolerate this and would often relegate the unwelcome one to the cities' outskirts to live in squalor. Some were even killed. But Christians took in many of these feebleminded.

The pagans were not totally without compassion, but they limited most of their charity to their own families. Christians introduced a radical notion: the spiritual family included all believers in Christ. And this enormous family extended its compassion to those outside it.

History repeats itself. Here we are in the twenty-first century, suddenly aware that in many parts of the world Christians are sold into slavery and treated brutally. And as in the Roman Empire, the faithful extend loving hands across the globe, rescuing people of faith from their persecutors. Whether the ancient Roman Empire or twenty-first-century Sudan, the response is the same: God's people "rescue those who are being taken away to death."

———

Resolution: Do some reading on the persecution of Christians in the world today. Find out what you can do to aid people who are perishing for their faith.

26

Quiet, Everyday Glory

Grandchildren are the crown of the aged,
and the glory of children is their fathers.

Proverbs 17:6

L IKE many people, I have made a hobby of tracing my family tree. No one of note is listed there. My father carried on the tradition; he was Mr. Average. After returning from the Korean War, he worked various jobs until, in the last years of his life, he was what we laughingly called "a professional killer"—a pest-control man. This is something I've always admitted quietly, for it is not something you trumpet.

Yet if one is a pest-control man, why not do it well, and with a good attitude? And so he did. At his visitation in the funeral home, we were amazed at how many of his customers dropped by. They all liked my dad, basing their opinion on the few minutes he was in each home to do his job and to chat for a moment before leaving. They said he was thorough, pleasant, thoughtful. Some stated that when they phoned the pest-control company, they would often request my dad, for some of the other workers were sloppy and slipshod.

The neighbors loved him. He would, they all said, "give you the shirt off his back." I saw tears in the eyes of one of the pallbearers, the man who lives across the road from the family. Did not Jesus commend such neighborly virtues? "Whoever wants to become great among you must be your servant" (Matt. 20:26 NIV).

Homely virtues are not the qualities that stir up admiration in a young man. Why couldn't I have had a father who was an executive, a professor, an author, or even a gentleman farmer? Why couldn't he show some ambition instead of taking off for the river with his rod and reel? A teenage boy wants to be proud of his old man. I wasn't— not until he began to die.

When the man is confined to his bed for good, his vocation becomes unimportant. A bedridden man might as well be a pest controller as a corporate mogul. Both are immobile, both face eternity, both need assistance merely to subsist. Death is a great leveler.

My father in his prime was not a hero to me. Could that same man, dying, be my hero? He was; his extended dying made me look at him not as a loser, but as a representative of what all of us are: fragile, dependent, teetering at every moment on the brink of the eternal. The dying person ceases to *do* and merely *is*. In the last year of my dad's earthly life, he *did* nothing, save lying in bed, talking a bit, and taking gradually less and less food. But he *was* many things while bedridden: kind, gentle, undemanding, and totally without grudges or bitterness.

Dad died heroically—meaning he died as well as he could. Nothing else could be asked of anyone. My father died well—quietly, unpretentiously, just as he had lived. In his unobtrusive way, he was a "glory" to me, his son.

Resolution: If your parents are living, give them a call or an e-mail today, or see them face to face if possible.

27

Nation Transformation

Righteousness exalts a nation,
but sin is a reproach to any people.

Proverbs 14:34

D ID you hear the joke about the Irish teetotaler? It isn't a joke, actually. There was such a man, a forgotten hero of the faith.

In the late 1800s drunkenness became a major problem on the U.S. frontier and in the growing cities. Liquor producers set up saloons at the entrances of mines and factories. In a day when workers received their pay in cash, it was not uncommon for a man to fritter away his week's wages at a saloon. As society became more urbanized and anonymous, it was easier for men, especially in cities, to sneak drinks throughout the day. Alcoholism increased, and this inevitably meant tragedy for any family that depended on the father's wages.

Christians took note of this and preached moderation. Some went further and insisted on total abstinence. The anti-liquor forces prevailed, and in 1919 the Eighteenth Amendment to the Constitution outlawed the manufacture and sale of liquor.

Consumption of booze did not cease. It merely went underground, easily obtainable in any location. Bootleggers grew pig-rich, speakeasies flourished, law officers accepted bribes (in money or liquor), and organized crime became a permanent fixture of American life. Prohibition seemed to be a failure, and Congress repealed it in 1933.

Of course, the Prohibitionists' intentions were noble: they wanted America free from the evils of alcohol abuse. Perhaps they were more effective in their early days, when they merely urged fellow Christians (and fellow Americans) toward moderation. Preaching and publishing can influence public opinion and bring about change; legislation can also, but people who are not on the bandwagon inevitably resent government coercion.

By contrast, consider this historical tidbit from Ireland, a nation with a reputation for hard drinking: Theobald Mathew (1790–1856), a Catholic monk, started a campaign for temperance. Mathew (the "Apostle of Temperance") well knew the devastating effects of alcohol abuse. But never did he push for nationally enforced abstinence. Instead, he encouraged "taking the pledge" for abstinence—strictly voluntary, with no stigma attached to refusing the pledge. He never claimed that abstinence was necessary for Christians. He claimed only that more abstainers—or at least *moderate* drinkers—would make a safer and happier Ireland.

This is exactly what occurred—not a complete turnaround in morals and public welfare, but at least a 45 percent decrease in liquor consumption. This was accomplished not through legislation but through preaching. *Persuasion, not legislative coercion.* Theobald Mathew seems to have followed the wiser course: Preach to individuals and groups; if their attitudes and behavior change, then society will change. A nation will be, as Proverbs says, "exalted" when individuals within it live righteous lives.

Resolution: Pray for the morals of your nation, then set people an example through your own life.

28

Hate-Filled Saints

The fear of the LORD is hatred of evil.
Pride and arrogance and the way of evil
and perverted speech I hate.

Proverbs 8:13

Is hate a bad thing? Not always, apparently. The word appears often in the Bible in a positive way: God hates evil, and so do godly people. In the oft-repeated words of my grandmother, "You don't hate *people*, you hate their *ways*." Proverbs is a very hate-full book—oozing rancor for human wickedness. It teaches us to love our enemies while despising their evil actions.

How do we act upon this hatred? One way is obvious enough: don't do the things we hate. This brings us to Jesus' Golden Rule: "Do to others as you would have them do to you" (Matt. 7:12 NIV), and its flip side, don't do things to people you would not want done to you. If you hate arrogance in people, be humble. If you hate lying and gossip, don't participate in either. If you hate dishonest business dealing, be scrupulous yourself. Frankly, the Bible's morality is amazingly simple: hate in yourself the things you hate in other people, cultivate in yourself the qualities you like in other people. It is very simple, very basic, and very difficult, for we are easily distracted from our own failings.

The summit of a man's moral development comes when he learns to judge himself as he judges others. It is fine for you to loathe your neighbor's greed and his spiteful tongue—so long as you can hate those same qualities in yourself. One crucial difference: you cannot change your neighbor, but you can change yourself. And giving sufficient attention to your own flaws is certainly the best—most godly—way to distract yourself from the faults of others.

The hourly news reminds us that the world is (as it always has been) a hate-filled place. One nation, tribe, ethnic group, or political group hates another, and the conflict leads to slander, violence, war, and terrorism. The hatred in Proverbs is a different sort altogether—not one of human groups or of human individuals, but one of evil in any form. We ought to hate evil as something that does not belong in human life, just as weeds do not belong in our gardens. And while we might detest the many weeds in our neighbors' gardens, the only proper place to begin weeding is in our own. Uprooting our own sins takes time and attention—so much that if we ever finished the task (which is unlikely), we would have no energy left to hate human beings.

Resolution: Make a list of behaviors and attitudes that you hate when you see them in other people. Consider which ones you are guilty of yourself. Resolve to direct your mind not to those faults in others, but those in yourself.

29

Pig Snouts and Sequins

Like a gold ring in a pig's snout
is a beautiful woman without discretion.

Proverbs 11:22

A GOOD friend of mine told me his story:

"Class reunions are happy, sad, eye-opening events. Mine was happy because I was seeing some people for the first time in twenty years. It was sad because some members of the class had passed on. It was eye-opening because I myself was older and wiser and saw both good and bad where I had not seen them before.

"Most of us had changed physically—some for the better, most not. But one who defied time was the girl—*woman*, now—I will call Sylvia. She was gorgeous. Wrinkle-free, tan, slim, and slinky, sporting a clingy sequined dress few of the other women would have dared to wear. She still had that hearty, earthy laugh, and she still chuckled easily at my jokes. (Oh, the things that stroke men's vanity!) On the dance floor, well, it was 1975 all over again, and if any of us had slowed down, lost our 'cool,' Sylvia had not.

"And yet . . . Sylvia introduced me to her boyfriend, father of her two children. She and the boyfriend had cohabited for fifteen years.

He had proposed marriage—but she refused. She explained, loud and brassily, 'Just 'cause I have two kids with a guy doesn't mean I have to change my name, right?' She was just as noisy and assertive about the child she did not have (she'd undergone an abortion—without mentioning it to the boyfriend beforehand). And she was her old mocking self: gossiping about class members who were not there (and some who were), mocking religion (she hated the church), mocking life in general, glad only that she was still blond and slender and 'her own person' with two kids that had *her* last name. What had been a trickle of swear words from her in the 1970s was now a flood.

"I think it safe to say that being seen—and envied—was the joy of Sylvia's life. Every woman in that room coveted her looks, but nothing else. Most of us had grown up and simmered down. Most had put aside that old agricultural pursuit of sowing wild oats. She had not.

"Had I grown old and serious and prudish? Or was I just astute enough to see that Sylvia had not wised up or grown up, but only grown coarse? Still beautiful in that sequined dress, and yet . . . why hadn't she, in twenty years, grown a heart or a conscience?"

"A gold ring in a pig's snout"—an ugly image, yes, but one that sums up a certain type of person very well. We should all, male or female, strive not to be such a person. Physical beauty without discretion and other spiritual qualities is not at all attractive.

———

Resolution: Think of physically beautiful people you know—both men and women. Are most of them nice people? Moral people? Does our culture emphasize physical attractiveness so much that beautiful people feel they can neglect the inner person?

30

Déjà Views

All the days of the afflicted are evil,
but the cheerful of heart has a continual feast.

Proverbs 15:15

THE closest I ever came to seeing "a continual feast" was at the home of my Uncle Earl and Aunt Ruth. I never knew a happier place. And it was not because of their possessions, for those were few. My uncle worked hard and steadily but never held a high-paying job. My aunt never worked—or more precisely, she worked full-time at raising their six children. (Obviously this was a more-than-full-time job, yet if it tired her, she never let on. Love is not whiny.) All her life was a kindness. She was as good as gold and as true as steel.

If you have had the pleasure of spending time with a large (multi-child) family, you know that they are usually happy. My six cousins lived in the most modest of homes (miraculously, eight people shared one bathroom), and compared with me, they had few toys as kids. But they were never bored. They enjoyed the most basic of human pleasures: each other. Fights and quarrels erupted but ended in a matter of minutes. No one held a grudge, and the size of the house did not allow for going to one's room and pouting. (No one had a room to himself.)

My aunt was not the best housekeeper. She couldn't be, since the house was as busy as a train station. She cooked well (as mothers of numerous children typically do), nothing fancy, but plentiful, simple, and hearty meals that she served up with generous portions of love and courtesy. If the floors were worn and scuffed, the drapes needed cleaning, or the kitchen needed a good scrubbing, what did it matter? And what did it matter if she never had new furniture to show off? A house was for living in, and they lived well, content with what they had.

In the course of time, all six kids married, and since none moved more than few miles away, they congregated every Sunday after church at "the home place." The house, never the type to be featured in *Better Homes and Gardens*, in time became a four-generation gathering place. Some people might have considered it "a dump"—but no one who spent time there ever did.

My aunt passed on and a few years later my uncle did as well. For a few more years the children, grandchildren, and great-grandchildren still gathered at the house on Sundays. It was not the same with my aunt and uncle gone, of course, but a house full of memories is a pleasant place to be. I loved that spot, that happy old home, which was like a dream I could never dream again. While they lived, their home was "a continual feast."

————

Resolution: Think of people you know who have few material possessions but who are happy and content. Do you enjoy the company of such people?

31

God, Pharaoh, and Mr. Heston

When the righteous thrive, the people rejoice;
when the wicked rule, the people groan.

Proverbs 29:2 (NIV)

T HOUGH it was released in the 1950s, the movie *The Ten Commandments* is still popular, and one of the few Hollywood classics that a major network reruns almost every year. And why not? The story is priceless—and timeless. Aside from its exotic setting in Egypt (extravagant sets and costumes), it has a powerful, hiss-worthy villain (the evil Pharaoh) facing a righteous man (Moses, played by Charlton Heston), and the power of the righteous, invisible God of Israel. In the background are thousands of oppressed Hebrew slaves, awaiting the outcome of the confrontation.

Evil never gives in easily, of course. Pharaoh was powerful—and obstinate. The Old Testament records that he "hardened" his heart against Moses and Israel (Exod. 7:14). God sent plague after plague upon the Egyptians, yet Pharaoh's heart remained steadfast. Even after he obeyed the divine command to "Let my people go!" Pharaoh changed his mind, pursued the freed slaves, and saw his soldiers drowned in the Red Sea.

The Book of Exodus—and the lavish movie—remind us that God can remove even the most deeply rooted evil.

If you are familiar with the Old Testament, you know that Moses is its most prominent character; more books mention him than any other person. Proverbs, however, doesn't mention Moses or the Exodus. Yet Proverbs has much to say about righteous and unrighteous rulers—and clearly its authors knew that the unrighteous were more numerous. (See Proverbs 14:34, 24:24, 29:18. Also, consider Psalm 146:3: "Do not put your trust in princes, in mortal men, who cannot save.") The world has never lacked for "mini-Pharaohs" who oppress people if they have the opportunity. Yet the God of Proverbs does not turn a blind eye to oppression and exploitation.

Evil will never be completely overcome in this world, of course. But God still holds out the eternal standard, a government where "the people rejoice" because "the righteous thrive."

———

Resolution: Pray for all government officials—not just heads of nations, but governors, judges, mayors, policemen, and prison workers. Pray they will be guided by God's standard of righteousness.

32

Poor Little Rich Folk

Riches do not profit in the day of wrath,
but righteousness delivers from death.

Proverbs 11:4

AUTHOR William Makepeace Thackeray ended his classic novel *Vanity Fair* with these words: "Which of us is happy in this life? Which of us has his desire, or, having it, is satisfied?"

Thackeray devoted eight hundred pages to showing how humorous—and how pathetic—it is when people, even those who consider themselves Christians, pursue riches and fame. We all know this, and the great Christian and non-Christian thinkers throughout the ages have repeated the theme. Yet we are preoccupied with material prosperity rather than with God himself. Eternity, the new humanity, the approaching heaven and earth where righteousness dwells—these we push aside in our thinking.

In the 1990s, American author Tom Wolfe wrote an updated version of *Vanity Fair*, the novel *A Man in Full*. Its central character, a wealthy Atlanta business mogul, faces his "day of wrath"—his comeuppance for all his years of dubious business deals. He and the other wealthy characters have one common trait: they are not at all happy.

But their money and possessions distract them from their spiritual emptiness—until a true crisis comes, that is.

Most of the time we do not feel spiritually hungry. We lose our spiritual appetite. We are not conscious of how greatly we need God. Christ, in Revelation, addressed severe words to the smug, satisfied church of Laodicea. "You say, I am rich, I have prospered, and I need nothing, not realizing that you are wretched, pitiable, poor, blind, and naked" (Rev. 3:17). The people there believed they had all they needed. But Christ assured them that they could not be filled until God himself filled them.

In *The Four Loves*, C. S. Lewis wrote, "Our whole being by its very nature is one vast need; incomplete, preparatory, empty yet cluttered, crying out for Him." How sad to be needful—but how much sadder to be empty and not know our condition. How tragic, with a deep spiritual craving at the center of our being, that we try to fill it with "toys"—cars, clothing, jewelry, vacations, the newest electronic gizmos.

God has promised to meet every need of his children. But this he cannot do until we recognize our need. Doing this, we need not worry about whether he will find us fit to receive his help.

Resolution: Ask yourself that classic question, what one possession would you want if stranded on a desert island? The Bible, maybe? Or could you maybe do without any possessions, so long as you were relying on God?

33

Belittle, and Be Little

A fool's mouth is his ruin,
and his lips are a snare to his soul.

Proverbs 18:7

COCKEYE" was the name we kids on the bus bestowed on the little blonde girl with one crossed eye and painfully thick glasses. She was probably about eight years old, myself about twelve. I say that "we kids" named her Cockeye, but I must admit that I myself was the first to use the word. The other kids picked up on it quickly, not because I was a natural leader but simply because it seemed cute and clever, and because the poor little girl had no older brother or sister to stand up for her. There on the crowded bus, for a few fleeting seconds, the other kids and I enjoyed our smirks and giggles at someone else's expense.

I should mention that this occurred at an age when I was active in my church and Sunday school, a star student, and someone teachers, pastors, and most other adults called a "good little boy." Being a "good little boy" can evoke serious persecution from other children, particularly from other boys, and I had endured my share.

It's quite possible that on the day I first called the blonde girl Cock-eye, I had received my own daily dose of verbal abuse.

According to the old song "Pass It On," we can pass on God's love to others. It is much easier to pass on abuse. It is pretty well documented that parents who physically mistreat their children were often mistreated themselves. Verbal abuse is likewise contagious, passed not only from parent to child, but from any abused person to another.

Of course, this doesn't explain why some people, those at the top of the pecking order, have never been verbally assaulted but freely dish it out. They aren't "passing it on"—they are doing it for the most basic reason of all: they enjoy it. It makes them feel good to hurt another human being and get away with it.

How many times have we heard kids say to the persecuted one, "We do it only because we like you"? Has anyone ever been stupid enough to believe this? I've always suspected it was a weasel phrase, something the persecutors say to the disapproving adult who is standing over them asking, "What's the matter with you kids? Why are you picking on her?" The honest answer would be "Because we enjoy it. It feels good."

By calling her Cockeye, I demoted her from stranger to less than human. I had taken pleasure in poking fun at a child's physical flaw. I didn't care if it hurt her feelings, if she cried after she got home, or if it had any repercussions on her life.

But today, I wish I knew where she lives. I would apologize if I could find her. She may have forgotten the teasing completely, but I have not.

———

Resolution: Think of people you may have injured with harsh words. If you can do so, contact them, let them know you were wrong.

34

Honoring God and Orphans

Whoever oppresses a poor man insults his Maker,
but he who is generous to the needy honors him.

Proverbs 14:31

THE Bible has a lot to say about God's love for society's outcasts—including orphans. And no wonder. Historically, the orphan's life was doomed to failure. People sold and traded them like goods. They maimed and dismembered some so that adult beggars could use them to elicit sympathy (and money) from passersby. In the 1700s, however, Christian concern for poor children led to the opening of orphanages that were more than just residences. They became vocational training schools as businesses and orphanages worked together to provide apprenticeships for willing youngsters. Note the change: instead of just giving food, clothing, and shelter to the children, these organizations gave a ladder out of poverty.

In the early 1700s the German Pietist August Hermann Francke started such a school for orphans, with both classroom and vocational training. The orphan school grew to have its own hospital, pharmacy, and printing press. Francke stressed the idea of educating poor kids so they wouldn't be poor adults.

At the same period in England, the Quakers acted as middlemen who found jobs for the unemployed. The Quakers were also noted for distributing food and clothing to the poor immediately after worship services—an example of bringing charity and worship together.

In time, most Christians (both Protestant and Catholic) came to believe that the poor could work themselves out of poverty—they could go not necessarily from rags to riches, but at least from rags to comfort. John Wesley and his Methodists discovered this in England in the 1700s. Few of the early Methodists were rich or even middle-class. (This was also true of the first Christians, by the way.) Ignored by the state-supported Church of England, many of the poor who came to hear Wesley preach had (to use a modern term) low self-esteem. Wesley took to the fields and mines, preached a pure gospel of love and forgiveness, and found people responding. Wesley's societies distributed food and clothing to the poor; material aid plus spiritual aid was a winning combination.

People who were poor could follow one of two paths after they prospered: they could hoard what they had and keep it to themselves, or they could remember what a burden poverty was and help the needy around them. Alas, there are far more people in the first category than in the second, human nature being what it is. But throughout the long history of Christianity, there are many shining examples of poor folk who turned their lives around (with the aid of God and godly people) and who in turn gave spiritual and material aid to the lowly. It is a spiritual "domino effect" that God approves. As the Proverb says, we honor our loving and generous God when we honor the people he created, including (especially) the poor.

———

Resolution: The next time you are tempted to splurge and buy an unnecessary item for yourself, take the money you would have spent on it and give it to a poor person.

35

When Silence Is Not Golden

A word fitly spoken
is like apples of gold in a setting of silver.

Proverbs 25:11

SILENCE, a proverb tells us, is golden. The Book of Proverbs has much to say about words spoken rashly. But can it ever be wrong to be silent? Most assuredly. I think the most painful experience of my own life involved an awkward silence on the part of people I believed were fellow Christians.

At the time my father died I was employed with a Christian ministry. Just before leaving for work one morning I received a phone call from my mother, telling me Dad had just passed away. Because the ministry I worked for had its own travel agency, I dropped by to pick up my plane ticket to fly home. While in the hallway I ran into a young man in my own department, a man I knew only slightly. He greeted me with a pleasant smile, then asked me jokingly why I wasn't wearing a tie. I replied, "My father just died this morning. I came here only to pick up my plane ticket."

There was an awkward and protracted pause, then finally a long "Ummm" from the young man, followed eventually by a chipper

"Well, you have a good day." He walked away quickly, no doubt feeling embarrassed, and leaving me feeling worse than ever.

I knew this young man to be a solid Christian family man, active in his church. While we weren't close friends, I would have expected a response that was, well, more Christian. Would it have been so difficult to have said, "Oh, I'm sorry" and given a soft pat on the shoulder? Or to have suggested a moment of prayer together in an empty conference room or even the men's room?

Several days later I was back at work. Our department held its weekly meeting, and by this time everyone knew why I had been absent for a few days. I recall being confronted with a roomful of smiling faces—smiling in that bland, mildly charitable, mildly sympathetic way that religious people have. The man who chaired the meeting said, "Welcome back"—but not a word about my father's death. This was particularly unusual since our meetings always ended with a time of prayer, not just for our work projects but for our personal needs as well. No one bothered to mention my loss. Not one word, only bland half-smiles.

These people who did not know what to say were not horrible, evil people. They intended no harm by what they did—or rather did *not* do. Yet they did harm. There are sins of omission as well as sins of commission.

One exception: a woman in another department, someone I barely knew, sent me a short note: "I will pray for you during this time of loss. As you grieve for your father, know that your heavenly Father loves you." Surely this was what the proverb meant about "apples of gold in a setting of silver."

———

Resolution: Think of people you know who have experienced some deep personal loss recently. Give them a kind word.

36

Traffic Artery

*Whoever is slow to anger is better than the mighty,
and he who rules his spirit than he who takes a city.*

Proverbs 16:32

EVERY old insight is perennially fresh. Our parents and grand-parents told us to take a deep breath and count to ten—slowly—when we got angry: "Control yourself, children." But not everyone paid attention. I know this, having witnessed a major accident—five cars, two deaths (including that of an infant), seven injuries, and damage to a couple of storefronts. One of the five cars was totaled. One of the injured persons was partially paralyzed, and may still be.

The accident was totally preventable and thoroughly pointless. Someone was in a hurry, someone coming from the other direction was in a hurry, and they not only paid the price for their impatience but took a couple of lives in the process. Of the two drivers who caused the accident, one was on his way to the beach, the other on her way to the beauty salon.

The judge and jury seemed to agree that neither of these trips was urgent, and both drivers did some jail time. But the at-fault drivers' testimonies in court were both laughable and sad. Both claimed to be "stressed out" and had long lists of reasons why. Since this has become an all-purpose alibi in our culture, I was pleased to see that the jury did not buy it.

The Bible has high praise for patience and self-control—more praise than for either wisdom or bravery. The Bible calls people to be God's diehards, enduring life's great and small disagreeables and coming out stronger for having persevered. While others are groaning, swearing, and creating additional stress for themselves, the patient person is quietly waiting out the trial of the moment.

Most of us do not know many patient people. Most of us do not know many saints, either—and the two (if you can find them) tend to be the same. The old proverb "God takes his time, while the devil is always in a hurry" is not in the Bible, but it fits perfectly. You could even amend it to "God's people take their time, while the devil's are always in a hurry."

My grandmother, the most patient person I have ever known, worked as a nurse for many years. I asked her why she never seems to lose her temper. She replied, "Bleeding from an artery is urgent. Not much else is. Most things can wait."

I thought about her words as I sat in my car watching a noisy muddle of police cars, ambulances, fire trucks, people in uniforms, people bleeding and bruised, people stopped in their vehicles because the traffic at a major intersection could not move. A five-car accident, caused because two people thought their tasks were as urgent as bleeding from an artery. Their lack of self-control led, ironically, to some literal bleeding. What might have been spared if these people in their mad and selfish rush had been "slow to anger"?

––––––––

Resolution: Count to ten—slowly—when angry, and remember that God's people are patient.

37

Brother Spite, Sister Malice

A righteous man is cautious in friendship,
but the way of the wicked leads them astray.

Proverbs 12:26 (NIV)

W HY do people enjoy gossip and put-downs? Because gossip and put-downs create togetherness, and togetherness is a wonderful thing. Most people, even those who consider themselves loners, enjoy companionship of some sort. God did not think it right for Adam to be alone, so he made him a companion. Given that these were the only two people in the world, it may have been the only time in human history that people had no one to gossip about or poke fun at. Poor Adam and Eve, reduced to talking about themselves, the world, and God—but not other people. No wonder the Garden of Eden was a paradise.

Out here in the post-Eden world, gossip and spiteful speech are shortcuts to companionship. When I gave the name Cockeye to a little cross-eyed blonde girl who rode my school bus, I created (however briefly) a moment of bonding with the other kids. Groupness is very important to children; they ache to belong, even if that involves casting aside kindness and common sense.

To that age-old question of exasperated parents, "If Billy jumped off the cliff, would you do it, too?" some kids (if they were honest) would respond, "Well, sure, if the other kids were doing it." To the question, "Why did you pick on that poor little girl?" the most obvious reply is, "Everyone else was doing it."

Aside from the pleasure of belittling someone, there was the pleasure of doing something *together*. Kids can enjoy sitting around a campfire singing "Kum Ba Yah," and the same kids can feel togetherness as they join together to call one kid "Fatty," "Skinny," "Airhead," or "Cockeye." In the joy of groupness the feelings of that persecuted child are completely forgotten, of course. *Who cares what she thinks? She is there only to provide us some amusement.*

Thankfully, many people grow out of this groupthink stage, becoming more self- or God-directed. But most of us never outgrow it completely. What others think matters to us—a lot. If people we admire or respect think a certain way, we are inclined to think that way as well. If we think one group of people is smart or chic, those people's way of thinking appeals to us. What they like, we like, and (what has the potential for harm), what they hate, we hate.

Nothing gives you more in common more quickly than finding out you dislike the same person. Groupthink built on liking the same things is fine—a good basis for Christian fellowship, in fact. But groupthink built on contempt and malice is another matter entirely.

———

Resolution: Take stock of your friends. Are you bound together by mutual likes and interests—or by a pleasure in gossiping and putting other people down?

38

Cannibal Sports

The memory of the righteous is a blessing,
but the name of the wicked will rot.

Proverbs 10:7

HISTORIANS delight in comparing the last days of Rome with our own times. Similarities are not hard to find, particularly in the area of entertainment. Romans liked spicy slice-of-life theatre, with ample nudity, live sexual acts, and the actual torturing of criminals on stage. Chariot racing was an obsession, and as with modern-day soccer matches, fans of rival factions often rioted. In one riot in A.D. 532, thirty thousand people were killed. Note the date: 532 was more than two hundred years *after* the Roman Empire had become (in theory, at least) Christian.

Worse than drama and racing were gladiatorial games. Combatants greeted the emperors by shouting, "We who are about to die salute you." Blood and brutality followed, making today's hockey and boxing matches seem like parlor games. Gladiators, most of whom were slaves, criminals, or prisoners of war, fought to the death (portrayed vividly in movies such as *Gladiator* and *Spartacus*). The bloody sand was raked over, and a new contest would begin. Such bloodbaths were not just for the dregs of society, but for everyone, including the emperors. Bodies fell in droves, and the Roman elite cheered.

From the time of Emperor Nero on, Christians were part of the spectacle. The famous cry "Christians to the lions!" is truth, not legend. When Christianity became legal in the year 312 under Emperor Constantine, Christian persecution ceased, but the games did not. Did the supposedly Christian emperors find the games disgusting and immoral? If they did, they never let on. Politically speaking, it wouldn't have been prudent. The gory games were a cherished Roman tradition.

Both before and after Constantine's conversion, Christians lamented the evil of Roman public amusements. One Christian author called the games "cannibal banquets for the soul." Other Christian leaders claimed that the public shedding of blood for sport encouraged crime and a general disdain for human life—which was no doubt true.

Even though many gladiators were convicted criminals under a death sentence, sensitive souls grieved that citizens enjoyed watching the butchery. Besides, some professional gladiators made a career out of public slaughter. In response, many churches refused baptism to a gladiator unless he changed professions, and some congregations refused Holy Communion to Christians who attended the games. The gladiator shows eventually ended because enough Christians, and people influenced by them, saw the games as the cruel, vulgar, inhumane entertainment that they were.

Who now remembers the names of the vile people who slaughtered each other in the arenas—and the vile people who applauded? As the verse from Proverbs said, the name of the wicked rotted.

———

Resolution: Make yourself read a biography of a genuinely saintly person.

39

Attila the Softy

A soft answer turns away wrath,
but a harsh word stirs up anger.

Proverbs 15:1

A SOFT answer can save an individual from a bloody nose—or a city from being burned. Centuries ago, the city of Rome faced waves of nasty invaders. One wave was the Huns, those savage fighters from central Asia, led by that short, vicious leader named Attila. The Huns swept over southeastern Europe and on into Italy. Not far outside of Rome, Attila met with the pope, Leo, who somehow persuaded the barbarian leader to withdraw. (Too bad no one had a video camera. That meeting must have been quite interesting.) We can safely assume that Leo had a "soft answer" that turned away Attila's wrath. The year was 452.

Three years later, the city faced another horde, the Vandals led by Gaiseric. Leo had less success with this leader and the Vandals spent two weeks plundering Rome, carrying off the valuables (including things the Romans had taken from the Jerusalem temple centuries earlier). But it could have been worse, and happily Leo somehow persuaded the Vandal leader not to burn the city. No wonder the

Catholic church made Leo a saint and still refers to him as Leo the Great. He not only was a powerful pope but also a master of the "soft answer."

You cannot read far in Proverbs without noticing its concern for wise use of the tongue. Most quarrels begin not with deeds but with words, and words help perpetuate those quarrels. We all know this, and we know that all the old cliches are shrewd. "Silence is golden." "Count to ten (slowly) before losing your temper." "If you can't say anything nice, say nothing at all." Proverbs 15:1 is also a cliche, but true, and neglected. Today's culture, which urges people to "let their feelings out" and "say what they feel," rarely encourages them to practice the soft answer.

Most of us will never have the opportunity to turn back an army of barbarian invaders. Our "soft answers" will be much less dramatic, having only the effect of maintaining cordial relations with family members, friends, neighbors, coworkers. But in a sense we are doing exactly what Pope Leo was doing: keeping the barbarians out—out of our own lives, that is.

It took courage for Leo to meet with the fearsome Attila. (He had no assurance that Attila would not kill him on the spot.) It also takes some courage to say no to our impulse to answer harsh words with more harsh words. It is easier to give in, to return nastiness for nastiness, to let the enemy set the rules of the game. It is easier, but wrong. And giving in makes our individual lives messier, and adds to the world's surplus of anger and ill will.

———

Resolution: Think of times that a "soft answer" has saved you from a fight, either physical or verbal. Think of other times that you gave in to the temptation to fight back with harsh words of your own.

40

Futureless Oppressors

Fret not yourself because of evildoers,
and be not envious of the wicked,
for the evil man has no future;
the lamp of the wicked will be put out.

Proverbs 24:19–20

ALL who desire to live a godly life in Christ Jesus will be persecuted" (2 Tim. 3:12). So said the apostle Paul, who spoke from his own rich (and often painful) experience. Christ himself was abused and executed by two forces working together: a pagan empire and an established religion that saw him as a heretic.

Like Jesus, Christians have suffered throughout history at the hands of unbelievers *and* the hands of "religious" people. It began in Acts: a Jewish mob stoned to death the saintly Stephen, making him the first Christian martyr (Acts 7). The wicked ruler Herod executed James, one of the apostles, with a sword, then slammed the apostle Peter in prison (Acts 12). According to tradition, most of the apostles died for the faith.

The sufferings of Christians under the pagan Roman Empire are well known. Sometimes the persecution was local and unofficial—

mobs harassing people who shamed and infuriated pagans by holding to higher moral standards. Sometimes emperors, like the monstrous Nero, ordered the brutalities; he had Christians crucified and torn to shreds by wild beasts in the arena as pagan audiences applauded.

With the conversion of Emperor Constantine in A.D. 313, Christianity quickly changed from a persecuted minority cult to a respectable religion with the Roman Empire's sponsorship.

So did persecution end? Hardly. A new form arose: instead of pagans persecuting Christians, the established church began persecuting heretics. The problem: many of the "heretics" were in fact faithful Christians who took the Bible seriously and contrasted biblical faith with the power and worldliness of the "official church."

One example from the Middle Ages: the Waldensians, who were widely admired—and persecuted. Beginning in the 1100s in southern France, this group, which called itself "the Poor in Spirit," preached a return to the pure gospel of the New Testament: owning little, experiencing inner conversion, aiding the poor, living as the apostles lived. The contrast between this simple Christianity and the worldliness and corruption of the official church was obvious to everyone. Using the Inquisition as its heresy-hunting machine, the church authorities threw many of the Waldensians in prison and burned some at the stake, though the movement survived and still exists.

In more recent times, people of faith have suffered greatly under Communist regimes as well as militant Islamic governments—proving that people of no faith and of deep faith can persecute the godly. Yet the persecuted folk of today have the same assurance as Christ's first apostles: "The evil man has no future; / the lamp of the wicked will be put out." Even if the persecutors seem to triumph in this world, God's faithful ones will survive and thrive throughout eternity.

Resolution: Make a point of praying daily for people of faith who suffer persecution.

41

The Dog and the Cider

Like a dog that returns to his vomit
is a fool who repeats his folly.

Proverbs 26:11

THERE is nothing pretty or poetic about this proverb. It is disgustingly blunt, and it sticks in the mind. Even the most devoted dog-lovers in the world know that the animals do have this loathsome habit of heaving up their food—and eating it again. This is not only disgusting, but useless, for whatever soured on the dog's stomach once will do it again.

When you read this proverb, keep in mind the ancient world's view of dogs. They were not adored family pets, but mangy, mongrel street scavengers—nuisances and eyesores. In the Near East today, calling someone a "dog" is still a supreme insult. When Proverbs 26:11 compared fools to dogs, the image would have had an impact, even without mentioning the vomit.

Several years ago I sat in a charming pub in Northern Ireland, soaking up the local atmosphere. I soaked up other things and later learned to my chagrin that pub cider is very *hard* cider. It went down as sweet, bubbly apple juice, but it had a "sting," and the next morning I prayed to God either to ease my pain or let me die. Hangovers are memorable experiences (in the worst way), and anyone who ever experienced one would be a fool to let it happen again. But the world is full of fools, whose brains are much larger than those of dogs, but who act no wiser.

The ancient Greeks related the myth of Sisyphus, a man who was punished by being forced to roll a huge boulder up a hill, only to have it roll down again every time. Sisyphus was *forced* to repeat his fruitless act, yet the world is full of people who *choose* to do such things. "This darn thing rolls back down every time, but maybe this time will be different."

Some wise person defined *insanity* as repeating a behavior that one knows to be futile or harmful. Drink too much, get a hangover—and do it again. Cheat on one's spouse, cause grief at home—and do it again. Do harm to oneself, suffer the consequences—and do it again. Call it insanity. Call it folly, as Proverbs does. Experience is the best—and most painful—teacher, but fools are not willing to be taught, not even by their own painful memories. "This hurt me before, but maybe this time it will be different." God endowed his creatures with brains—and with the free will not to use the brain.

Too bad every sin does not lead to a hangover. There would be much less sin in the world.

———

Resolution: Focus on some behavior that you have repeated for years, something that has either done you harm or has proved useless, or both. Resolve to be "a wised-up dog," and cease that behavior.

42

Shutting Down
a Stubborn Mind

Trust in the LORD with all your heart,
and do not lean on your own understanding.

Proverbs 3:5

According to the slogan, "A mind is a terrible thing to waste."
It is also a terrible thing to rely on in every situation. The sad
truth is, even the most brilliant people can be wrong and misguided.
That is why the Book of Proverbs tells us to seek out people who are
wise—but to put our ultimate trust only in God. Consider these passages: "The way of a fool is right in his own eyes, but a wise man listens to advice" (12:15). "Pride only breeds quarrels, but wisdom is
found in those who take advice" (13:10, NIV). "Listen to advice and
accept instruction, that you may gain wisdom" (19:20). But never
forget 3:5: It is only the Lord that we should trust *with all our hearts*.

Had I relied on my own mind, I would never have learned to
swim. I regret to say that I did not learn until I was almost thirteen.
Somehow I had convinced myself that if my head ever went under

the water, I would die immediately. So I had to persuade myself once and for all that my body would indeed stay afloat. Everyone had told me so, and when I finally stopped my wild thrashing and started a more effective dog paddling, I knew the truth: water can indeed support the human body. And if your head goes under, fine — you simply don't breathe in for those few moments.

God made the water, God made the human body, God made us to frolic in the water and enjoy it. So adults had told me for years. But I had "leaned on my own understanding" and deprived myself of one of life's great innocent pleasures.

Once I was convinced, I never faltered. I wish I could say this was always true of my faith journey. Once, at a very memorable moment, I made a commitment to God, basing my decision on the testimony of others and on the need to love God and serve God. While I have never forgotten that commitment, I have sometimes acted as if my dedication had no effect on me. I have not trusted in the Lord with all of my heart; I have too often leaned on my own understanding.

I am glad God accepts us in our faltering attempts to lead lives of faith. I am glad there are believers whose dedication exceeds mine, for I need the daily encouragement of those whose conviction seldom wavers. I am glad there is a Father whose compassion and wisdom exceed those of even the best human counselors. I am glad my destiny in this world and the next is not dependent on my own limited understanding.

———

Resolution: Think of times in the past when you were truly misguided about something. What changed your mind and set you right? Friends? Family members? The Bible? Can you see God working through all of those?

43

Embraceable Blessing

Whoever brings blessing will be enriched,
and one who waters will himself be watered.

Proverbs 11:25

THE bumper stickers that asked "Have you hugged your kid today?" were trendy; they disappeared, then reappeared. Apparently hugging is still "in." Why all this concern about it? Maybe because in a world where physical intimacy seems so easy to come by—at least on a short-term basis—the warmth and innocence of an affirming hug is not such a common thing. Couples unite, bond temporarily, and then part, but even the media, with all its glorification of "liberation from repression," acknowledge the emptiness of what often passes for intimacy. Sexual activity does not solve the problem of loneliness.

For that matter, neither does hugging. But there's much to be said for an action that communicates this message: "I love you, care about you, and right now want nothing more from you than your presence." So many men and women fear waking up alone in the morning. Rather we should fear that we reach a point where the hug and its message are no longer true for us. We do well to fear that, after all the chatter about intimacy and freedom has ended, there is no real tenderness in our lives. We fail when we merely talk about tenderness. It must be concrete.

I sat at dinner recently with a college friend who, by normal standards, is doing well in life. She just made an upward job change, bought a new home, and finished paying off her car. She dresses well, talks cleverly and intelligently. But she is desperately lonely. I embarrass easily in public places, and I was extremely uncomfortable as she stared at me across the table and her eyes overflowed with tears. "Steve, why won't someone just hug me and tell me they *like* me?" I stepped out of character and did just that, right there in the restaurant. I don't think I solved her problem, but playing a small part is better than playing no part at all.

The story is told of philosopher Martin Buber embracing a surly New York cab driver and profoundly shocking the man. No one knows if the driver's life changed significantly. No one knows for sure—not even the psychologists with their figures on "hug quotas"—just how much good a hug can do. Buber did what seemed essential at the time, and so did I, and so do many other people.

We worship a loving God who, alas, cannot wrap his arms around us and squeeze comfort and hope into our aching hearts. He's left hugging to us humans. For those of us who are not particularly "touchy" by nature, it does not come easily. Yet hugs, like kind and loving words, are part of the promise of Proverbs 11:25: "Whoever brings blessing will be enriched, / and one who waters will himself be watered."

————

Resolution: Hug someone.

44

A Tough / Loving Father

*My son, do not despise the LORD's discipline
or be weary of his reproof,
for the LORD reproves him whom he loves,
as a father the son in whom he delights.*

Proverbs 3:11–12

JESUS, speaking to his disciples about what fate would befall them, painted a grim picture: "You will be hated by all for my name's sake. But the one who endures to the end will be saved" (Mark 13:13). He bound up the promise of salvation with the idea of persecution and suffering. Jesus gave the disciples a fair warning: expect salvation *and* tough times.

This has never been an attractive teaching. No one enjoys suffering. Yet, as the whole New Testament declares, it is part and parcel of the life of faith. If there is no hardship, if we are ever the secure and satisfied ones, we may need to reflect on our situation, because the state of painlessness is not the condition of God's children. The Epistle to the Hebrews states the matter with a startling directness: If we are not disciplined through hardship, we are illegitimate children. God trains and educates every true son or daughter by allowing each to endure pain and sorrow (Heb. 12:5–8).

Our modern notions of parental discipline run counter to the biblical concept of parenthood, which assumes that real love for a child involves discipline, not indulgence. But even modern Christians know that behind the Lord's discipline lie purpose and love.

The word translated "discipline" in Hebrews 12 is the Greek *paideia*, which can also be translated "instruction" or "training." The Greek word does not convey the concept of quiet, meditative learning; rather to endure *paideia* is to undergo the regular drilling needed to prepare one to face life in the adult world. The rigorous training of the young boys of ancient Sparta may be the extreme example of *paideia*.

According to this passage, God, like all good human parents, uses discipline to train us for life. Human fathers prepare their children for the adult world, while God, who watches over the individual's ultimate destiny, employs discipline to achieve a life of holiness that is a manifestation of the present and coming kingdom.

We do not particularly like *paideia*. We tend to think that our faith should be a soft flannel blanket that never scratches. But we cannot expect such treatment from God, who is Parent, Teacher, and Trainer. The experienced trainer knows that there is no reaching the goal unless life's hardships produce in us personal humility and fortitude of soul.

Resolution: Pray that God will help you recognize in the hardships of life the love that undergirds the training that prepares us for his kingdom.

45

Free Me from Me

Many are the plans in the mind of a man,
but it is the purpose of the LORD that will stand.

Proverbs 19:21

SELF is the name of a popular magazine. In fact, looking at the magazines at the grocery checkout, you might think that *self* is the theme of all of them. They appeal to ego, and it is an easy appeal. We naturally—inevitably—want to read something that will tell us how to look prettier, live longer, reduce stress and pain. We inevitably are interested in "getting in touch with ourselves."

And just as inevitably, we yearn for independence. Children at a younger and younger age free themselves from parental restrictions. Husbands and wives work out arrangements for spending time apart, with the wife sometimes keeping her maiden name to prove her independence. Lovers go their separate ways when one or the other begins to feel "cramped." Something in us drives us to be islands, and even when lust or loneliness drives us back toward human companionship, we want it on our own terms, with few attachments and few responsibilities.

But selfishness is tiresome. We have all known people who are truly independent, truly self-sufficient, yet they are not "together." They are in their own hell, so bound up in their own egos they cannot truly love. It is impossible for them to see around the corner of themselves.

Selfishness is a burden. In the world's view, each person should "look after Number One," pursuing his own goals and plans regardless of anyone else's needs. But the pursuit is too much for any human being to bear. Even the healthiest, wealthiest, most successful individual cannot endure the strain of being fully responsible for his own life. Even the greatest must face the awkward questions: *What happens if my money or health goes? What happens when I die?*

In the world of inevitability, these questions have no answer. But people of faith have an answer: Depend on the Father. Submit to Someone greater than yourself. Be willing to lose your life, for only then will you have the life that endures. "Whoever seeks to preserve his life will lose it, but whoever loses his life will keep it" (Luke 17:33). This is not the world's way, but God's way—freedom from self.

Back to Proverbs 19:21; we make our selfish plans, and we spend our lives among other people trying to work out their own selfish plans. But Someone bigger and better than ourselves is at work in the universe, thankfully, and his ultimate plan for the world will succeed. We can only imagine what the world would be like if each of us actually achieve our selfish desires. It would not be a pretty place. So be glad God is in charge of it all.

Resolution: Begin the day by committing yourself and all your plans to God. Promise yourself, and God, to avoid worry.

46

Healthy, Beautiful, Unhappy Folk

There are those who are clean in their own eyes
but are not washed of their filth.

Proverbs 30:12

*S*IN has become "the S word," the word that polite company doesn't speak. It conjures up images of old-fashioned intolerance that the world will not tolerate.

But the idea of sin won't go away. Somehow we all—even people who would never use the word *sin*—sense that something is wrong with human beings, as a whole and as individuals. What is it that's amiss? We look for any answer to that question rather than the real one: we are selfish, we like to play God, we like to be the center of the universe, we fail to honor and obey the true Center of the universe. That is what sin is.

We accept less honest answers: We are overweight. We are out of shape. We are oppressed by a higher economic class. We are the victims of prejudice. We are not in the right job. We are not married to (or dating) the right person. Something is lacking, and we believe that somehow we can correct it ourselves.

But humanly speaking, we cannot. We may improve ourselves in some way, but we can't fundamentally change what's wrong. Our self-centeredness stands between us and the one who made us. Until we correct the old sin problem, nothing else will help much.

How can we do that? Do we take our own punishment for sin? Not according to the Bible: Jesus "was delivered over to death for our sins and was raised to life for our justification" (Rom. 4:25, NIV). "Justification" means *made right.* That anxious feeling that all human beings experience—the feeling we are not quite right—can be dispelled. Jesus died on the cross in our place. He rose from the dead. He offers us release from the nagging certainty that we are less than we should be.

Believers are "set free from sin" (Rom. 6:18 NIV). Does this mean that Jesus' followers *never* sin? Hardly. It does mean that we are no longer the slaves of sin. We serve a new Master, the one who gives freedom from the need to do self-serving and destructive things, from trying to save ourselves.

Proverbs 30:12 reminds us that some people are "clean in their own eyes." They "eat right," exercise, lower their cholesterol, and manage (temporarily) not to show the effects of aging. They "take care of themselves" physically and neglect the more important spiritual issue: the "filth," the pride and selfishness that mar their relationships with God and with other people. No one has yet devised a diet or exercise program that will tackle that fundamental problem.

———

Resolution: Think back on the various "self-improvement" plans you may have tried over the years—diets, exercise programs, whatever. Did they, in any deep sense, improve your life?

47

Valley of the Shadow

The fear of man lays a snare,
but whoever trusts in the LORD is safe.

Proverbs 29:25

SEVERAL years ago, singer Anne Murray crooned a song about how we "sure could use a little good news today." If she was expecting the news media to start focusing on the positive, she was much too optimistic. The media accentuate the negative, and apparently that is what the people expect. Your TV newscast and daily newspaper are not bearers of good cheer.

Listening to environmental doomsayers, you will hear that the earth is dangerously warming. (A few years ago they predicted we were entering another Ice Age, so obviously the "experts" can change their tune.) Thanks to humans' abuses, they say, the earth may soon become uninhabitable. But even if the air and water hold out, the threat of terrorism hangs over all of us. Crime takes its toll. Taxes increase. Leaders are greedy and corrupt. "Stable" investments can lose their value overnight. Families, long considered the main source of our stability, break apart.

Even if we console ourselves with some simple historical analysis (crime, taxes, corruption, war, and the like have always existed) and with the fact that the environmentalists aren't always correct, we still worry that the good life will elude us.

Fear is real. In a world where the media bombard us with images of certain destruction, we *must* be afraid. More and more people suffer from insomnia, as all the doctors and pharmacists know. They lie in bed, worried that this earthly life, the only life they can believe in, will not be the featherbed existence they had expected. What will save us? Politicians? The latest social program? The arms buildup? Peace marches?

Only the God who raises the dead sets us free from fear. We do not have to believe that this earthly life is all. In fact, we are certain it is not. That does not mean that we treat it lightly, but it is not our final priority—or our final hope. Biological life is less important than eternal life in the presence of God.

Global warming, nuclear and biological warfare, terrorism, crime, and economic recession are serious and frightening, but they are not the last word. "Neither death nor life, nor angels nor rulers, nor things present nor things to come, nor powers, nor height nor depth, nor anything else in all creation, will be able to separate us from the love of God in Christ Jesus" (Rom. 8:38–39).

"Whoever trusts in the Lord is safe," says the proverb. None of the things that threaten us—terrorists, corrupt politicians or financiers, nothing—is bigger than God.

———

Resolution: For a day (or longer, if you can bear it), try a "news fast." Give yourself a complete break from news on the radio, TV, or newspapers.

48

Stuck in Idol Mode

There is a way that seems right to a man,
but its end is the way to death.

Proverbs 14:12

YEARS ago, Coca-Cola ran an ad campaign with the slogan "Coke—it's the real thing." Before long someone had printed bumper stickers with "God—the real thing." You might say that that bumper sticker summed up the whole message of the Bible.

One idea that saturates every page of the Bible is this: *Do not worship false gods.* In the Old Testament, this meant not bowing down to the idols of Egypt, Canaan, and the other nations. What these countries called *sacred,* God's people called *empty* and *useless.* When God gave Israel the first of the Ten Commandments ("You shall have no other gods before me"—Exod. 20:3), he was freeing them from worshiping lifeless idols, gods that were not gods at all.

You may have heard that the modern world is secular, not religious. You might believe that educated, enlightened people in the twenty-first century have no sense of the sacred. It isn't so. As the Bob Dylan song of several years ago said, "You gotta serve somebody," and if that somebody is not God, it is some other god. Drop by your local health club and observe the worship of the god of Youth. Watch the TV ads and see that people widely reverence Beauty and Money (called "Mammon" in the Bible—these gods are not new). Society treats these matters with a seriousness—and with time, money, and energy—that human beings should apply only to what is sacred.

We also deify things such as Privacy (we believe that what we do is no one else's business) and Choice (we want to be able to choose our own path, even if it's wrong). And Sex, the cure for all ills, is the pleasure that we apparently value above all others. (The Greeks called him Eros, and they knew he was a most powerful god.) And perhaps the most-worshiped idol of all is Self—which, when you think about it, is a foolish object of awe and service, a collection of flesh that will probably live only eighty years or so.

The time, money, and mental energy that people expend on these false gods can only be called worship. Living among the worshipers of these gods, it is almost inevitable that we, too, must worship them. But we don't have to. We are free. In a world where a crucified carpenter can rise from the dead, anything is possible. We can laugh at the false gods. We can turn away from the pursuit of gain. We can laugh at vanity and the endless round of seduction and disenchantment. In this world, people inevitably worship what is not God. But in the new world, a world where the dead are raised to life, we are free to worship the true God.

The pursuit of all the false gods "seems right to a man," as the proverb puts it, "but its end is the way to death." None of the false gods endures and none can ensure our eternal survival and happiness. Only the true God can do that.

Resolution: Ask yourself, What things do I hold sacred? How much energy and time do I devote to these things? How much do they distract me from the true God?

49

Agape Connection

Many a man proclaims his own steadfast love,
but a faithful man who can find?

Proverbs 20:6

IN the world today *sin* may be the unspeakable "*S* word," but the "*L* word," *love*, is one we constantly use. What does it mean? The fleeting attraction of one attractive body for another? The indulgent heaping of toys on a spoiled child? Something that we conjure up by sharing sunsets and candlelit dinners? Something that can be arranged quickly on TV's *Love Connection*?

In our world, for most people, this is what love means. Love is a commodity, something we can buy, sell, bargain for, trade. It is something to be acquired, like success, prestige, security, fame. In these uses, "love" is selfish. It is based on the old Greek word *eros*—love rooted in attraction and satisfying self. Writing about love, the New Testament authors deliberately avoided using *eros* and instead used *agape*, meaning an unselfish, nurturing, enduring love—the kind of love God himself shows.

"Greater love has no one than this, that he lay down his life for his friends" (John 15:13, NIV). The love Jesus was speaking of was this kind of love: *others*-centered, the love he himself showed by dying a criminal's death he did not deserve. This kind of love is not "normal." It is, in this world, surprising, shocking—it even seems impossible. But for people of faith, the impossible is possible. A self-centered human being can learn to see himself not in isolation, but only in relation to others.

That is real love, the *agape* Paul described so beautifully in the famous "love chapter," 1 Corinthians 13. It is still read at many weddings, though considering the high rate of divorce, we have to wonder how seriously many brides and grooms heed Paul's words: "Love bears all things, believes all things, hopes all things, endures all things. Love never ends" (1 Cor. 13:7–8).

No, *agape* never ends, but *eros* certainly does. The person who seemed so beautiful and enchanting on dates turns out to be childishly selfish, constantly thinking *my* instead of *our*. The disillusioned spouses move on and repeat their *eros* chase, sometimes for an entire lifetime, and no one benefits except the divorce lawyers and the companies that hawk their products to people who prefer the tediousness and shallowness of dating to the stability of a committed relationship.

As Proverbs has it, many proclaim their steadfast love, but how many really faithful lovers are there in this love-obsessed, self-obsessed world?

———

Resolution: Think of people you know who are genuinely loving— not just to their spouses and children, but to people in general. Are they people of faith?

50

The Cat in the Moon

A tranquil heart gives life to the flesh,
but envy makes the bones rot.

Proverbs 14:30

Bᴀᴄᴋ in the 1960s, with the world's attention focused on putting a man on the moon, some of us learned of a location we had never heard of before: the Sea of Tranquility. I loved that name from the first time I heard it. In fact, I rather love the word *tranquil*, one of those words that sounds like what it is. The Sea of Tranquility sounded like a perfect place to be, even if it was on the cold, silent moon.

Human beings are not, by nature, tranquil. Many animals are, which is one reason we are drawn to them. My cat is like almost all cats—very lazy and very peaceful. She is rare in one respect: she does not object to riding in a car. I carry her with me, she lies peacefully in my lap, and her calmness has a calming effect on me, which I desperately need considering our local drivers. I am convinced that if other drivers went about with cats in their laps, driving would be much less hectic.

Much of what destroys our tranquility is of our own making. As

Proverbs 14:30 states, one great destroyer is envy. Most people misunderstand envy. It is not a matter of "I want that!" but more a matter of "He has it and I don't!" Think back to the Ten Commandments: the tenth one does not say "You shall not desire things" but "You shall not covet your *neighbor's* house, wife, servant, ox," and so on (see Exod. 20:17). Envy and covetousness are a slap at God's justice, our doubting that he has distributed his gifts fairly. What disturbs our tranquility—"rots the bones," as Proverbs put it—is a human trait. My cat could not care less if the cat next door eats more expensive food. Only we humans envy, and only we are made unhappy by pondering what others have.

There is always some product or service—"new and improved"—to make life better (or so the promise), and someone we know already has that product. With all respect to capitalism (which is not a bad system in itself), the engine that runs it is envy, and envy itself is a bad thing.

The secret would be our learning to say, truthfully, "I rejoice in what I have and don't fret for what I haven't." Either we reset our expectations, or we condemn ourselves to perpetual disappointment. Someone will always be richer, stronger, handsomer. Other people's success (in strictly worldly terms, that is) is not what destroys our peace. Only our envy does. And envy is self-generated. We can envy—or choose not to. That is the way to tranquility.

Resolution: Think of things your acquaintances have acquired in the past few months. How did you react when they told you of their new purchases? Were you happy for them? Envious? Both? Were any of these products things you did not particularly need—but wanted because someone you know owned them?

51

Mocking the Cynics

He mocks proud mockers
but gives grace to the humble.

Proverbs 3:34 (NIV)

C YNICISM is hard to define but fairly easy to recognize. It involves a refusal to trust—anything or anyone. It becomes a habit, a sort of reflex as unconscious as blinking.

I know about cynics because I was one myself. Even though I attended a Christian college (so it was called), I couldn't help but absorb the prevailing attitude of college kids, namely cynicism. Peer pressure is a powerful thing, particularly to people of college age, and if your classmates tend to be snide and flippant and smirking in their conversations, you tend that way yourself. And throughout these years it has been a constant battle, since I dwell among peers, acquaintances, and neighbors who live and breathe the air of cynicism. I still struggle with it.

Consider the realities today's young people face, the life situations that are the seedbed of cynicism: broken families, parents with no belief in God or spiritual values, media filled with violence, greed, and sex that is rooted in nothing but selfishness. I suspect most of you grew up like myself, trained by the public schools to be patriotic. We knew our leaders were human, but we were taught to honor and respect them. Watergate (and the scandals since then) pretty much killed old-style patriotism. No wonder we began to look for, and expect, the bad in life.

The symptoms of cynicism are common enough: refusal to open up; crude behavior; a deep-seated loneliness glazed over with apparent indifference and independence; deliberate avoidance of spiritual concerns or anything that gives tenderness and meaning to life. The people who made a megahit out of Tina Turner's cynical "What's Love Got to Do with It?" can only snicker at the romantic songs that made stars of Perry Como and Doris Day.

Sarcasm is another symptom. This is obvious even in television programs tailored for children. It runs rampant in every form of comedy. Stand-up comedians once spouted questionable jokes about ethnic groups. But they told them with a kind of disarming, offhanded warmth. Now comedians don't belittle ethnic minorities; they are cynical about the whole human race, about life in general, and they scoff at their audiences. And the audiences keep paying for it—not just in money, but in an increase in their own cynicism.

Cynics live as if God were absent from life, and they protect themselves from their "Godforsaken" world with layers of negatives.

You won't find the word *cynic* in most Bibles. But "mocker," which has almost the same meaning, occurs often. Cynics and mockers have this in common: they love to sneer, and they are not happy people. They accentuate the negative. God calls his people to something higher, something positive, something eternal. After all, we know that this world is not, in spite of all the badness, a Godforsaken place.

————

Resolution: In this cynical world, pray daily to keep yourself untarnished.

52

Wising Up the Scholar

Be not wise in your own eyes;
fear the LORD, and turn away from evil.

Proverbs 3:7

GOD, I thank you that I am not like other men. . . ." So began the prayer of the self-righteous Pharisee in Jesus' famous parable (Luke 18:9–14). Spiritual pride takes different forms. The Pharisee looked down on robbers, evildoers, adulterers. In my college days, I looked down on Grand Ole Opry fans, Louis L'Amour fans, the uneducated, the "unenlightened." I had to go no further than my own home to find a prime example of Dull- and Backwardness. "God, I thank you that I am not like these semiliterate, uncultured men—like my father."

We may not, like the Pharisee, judge others' morals, but we can just as easily judge their speech, education, dress, manners. It is pleasant to think such thoughts—but hardly constructive to good family relations, and hardly conducive to one's spiritual growth. I was getting an A in every theology and Bible class and felt my professors appreciated me. At the same time, I snickered at seeing my dad in his undershirt on the porch, reading a Western.

Theology and Bible classes should make us appreciate God. But becoming (in our own eyes) wise and cultured can make us appreciate ourselves—we can *become* gods, high and lifted up, wise, looking down on the human race, especially those closest to us, for we well know their failings. "Why do you see the speck that is in your brother's eye and do not notice the log that is in your own eye?" (Luke 6:41) Why? Because we feel godlike when we place ourselves beyond judgment.

In the parable, the tax collector, whom the satisfied Pharisee loathed, beat his breast and said, "God, have mercy on me, a sinner" (Luke 18:13 NIV). My father was a sinner, my professors were sinners, and I was and am a sinner. That binds us all together, sons of Adam, fallen creatures needing redemption. Whether we listen to the Opry or the opera, we need a Savior.

My reconciliation with my father came in 1982, when he nearly died of double pneumonia. I recall standing by his bed in intensive care, feeling as uncomfortable from guilt as he did from sickness. Confronted with that nearly breathless body, I could not play the role of Pharisee: "I thank you, God, that I am wiser and more cultured than this man"—no, such words do not apply in such situations, nor should such words ever enter our minds. "I love you, Dad" and "I'm here if you need me"—those words stuck in my throat, but they came out as I recalled the important fact: this was my father, the earthly authority God gave me to love and honor. I had not honored him as I should, and I could not give him back the years in which I judged him harshly. But I could love him in his illness, as I loved him through the 1991 illness that ended his earthly life.

Everyone who knew my father loved him. I loved him as a child, looked down on him as a collegian, and loved him again in his last years, finding myself praying the tax collector's prayer and not the prayer of the Pharisee.

———

Resolution: Think of people you have made a habit of looking down on. Make a point of reaching out to these people with a friendly word or smile.

53

When "Together" Breaks Apart

Do not boast about tomorrow,
for you do not know what a day may bring.

Proverbs 27:1

SOMETIME in the 1990s the expression *control freak* entered the American vocabulary. A control freak was someone who had to have everything his way, someone who did not feel comfortable unless he was on top of every situation. By that definition, each of us is a control freak. Left to our own devices, we would have everything in our lives "just so"—which is impossible, since each person's arrangement of "just so" would not fit with anyone else's.

Still, all of us wish to order and control our destinies as much as possible. And why not? God gave us minds, wills, the ability (which animals lack) to see and conceive of the future. Wanting to control our lives is, you might say, showing we are made in God's image.

Where we go astray, however, is not in planning ahead, but in assuming reality will shape itself according to our plans. We "boast about tomorrow," to use the phrase from Proverbs. God gave us the power to make plans—and also the power to bend (or break) when the plans are changed.

In my younger days I shared an apartment with a young graduate student who was, by worldly standards, totally "together." He was handsome, brilliant, and charming. He was studying computer science, with a hefty scholarship paying for his entire education. He had every reason to assume his future would be perfect: a high-paying job, social prestige, probably a beautiful wife, an impressive home (or homes), a country club life, a life of ease. Even in his first year of graduate school he was already exploring major corporations with which he might take a job. Whenever he went on a date, he could practically make the woman swoon, not just with his present assets (looks and brains) but future assets (money and prestige).

One night he left our apartment for a dinner meeting and never came back. He was involved in a three-car accident. His legs were seriously injured, as was his face. For several weeks he was only half-conscious, so his academic year came to an abrupt end. His family had to take his belongings from the apartment. The last they told me, he had had some plastic surgery on his face but still had some severe scarring. They feared it would take years of therapy before he could concentrate on school again, and the college would not hold the scholarship.

A punishment from God for pride and arrogance? I don't like to think so. And yet, such events remind us that we ourselves are not in control of our future and so we cannot boast. Who among us knows what tomorrow—or the next minute—will bring?

————

Resolution: Think of plans you have made over the years and how many of them never came to pass. Had it occurred to you at those times that you might have been arrogant and presumptuous, assuming they were guaranteed to come to pass?

54

Kickin' the Big Boys

Whoever utters slander is a fool.

Proverbs 10:18

WHEN it comes to gossip, particularly about celebrities, Christians are different—right? If only. After working with many believers over the years, I can honestly say that there is, overall, a difference. Christians generally gossip and belittle people less (and do so less maliciously). But *less* is a relative term. It is not the same as *never*. In fact, too often we appear to be conforming to the world's low standards.

I was working for a Christian organization in the 1980s when the Jim and Tammy Bakker scandal hit the national news. All of our employees were painfully aware of how the media perceived the Bakkers: "Christian hypocrites—but aren't they all?" Here were two Christian celebrities, cut down to size and darn near dehumanized by having their shady financial dealings revealed to the world. One of them (Jim) went to prison, the other (Tammy) became the butt of a million jokes, not because of the financial scandal but because of her looks and voice.

From a Christian perspective, the scandal should have been

something over which we wept. Every scandal like this gives God's enemies some extra ammunition. (Think of David's adultery with Bathsheba. The prophet Nathan told David that "by doing this you have made the enemies of the LORD show utter contempt"—2 Sam. 12:14 NIV.) The proper Christian response was to pray for the Bakkers (who, for all we knew, were merely two people of faith who had gone astray), then pray that some good might come of it all, with ministries being more circumspect in their financial dealings, more conscious of keeping their morals above reproach. (Thankfully, this did occur.)

But at the time we Christians snickered. I heard—and repeated—numerous jokes about the Bakkers. I doubt seriously that any secular workplace derived more mirth from their tragedy than the Christian company where I worked. (Perhaps our jokes were *cleaner*, but they were no less malicious.) Two well-known Christians had been caught with their hands in the cookie jar. Why not laugh about it?

For a few weeks, until we all got bored with the scandal, we experienced the joy of comparison—"I may not be the greatest Christian in the world, but I'm certainly not as bad as those Bakkers." Yet nothing the Bakkers did, bad as it was, made our own spiritual lives any richer—we were no better for thinking them worse.

"Why do you pass judgment on your brother? Or you, why do you despise your brother? For we will all stand before the judgment seat of God" (Rom. 14:10).

———

Resolution: Ask yourself what fellow believers have you gossiped about in the past week? Did you find yourselves making comparisons between their morals and your own? Their looks? Their bearing? What did you gain from these comparisons?

55

Chigger Children

One who is full loathes honey,
but to one who is hungry, everything bitter is sweet.

Proverbs 27:7

CHIGGERS, in case you didn't know, are tiny insect larvae that burrow under the skin and cause a noticeable itch. They are an expected part of a southern summer, and in my two seasons as a camp counselor, I took chiggers in stride. So did most of the kids at the camp—but not the upper-class and upper-middle-class children who turned whining and complaining into a high art form. These kids were much more irritating than the chiggers were.

Everything was wrong: the heat, humidity, mosquitoes, chiggers. Everything they loved was missing: TV, stereo, video games, microwaves, telephones. Why had their parents punished them by sending them off to this uncomfortable (and low-tech) camp? (One guess: the parents tired of the whining, too.)

By contrast, each summer we had one week of "charity kids"— poor kids some generous churches sponsored. These children were not without their problems. Certainly they did not dress or care for their hair and teeth as well as the rich kids. Yet they were remarkably free of complaints. Not having all the electronic gizmos and toys at home, they did not miss them. They didn't mind manual labor (we all took turns cooking over an open fire and washing dishes). "Camp grub" was just fine with them. Best of all, sleeping out in the woods, they didn't whine much about the chiggers and mosquitoes.

Occasionally I run into one of my fellow camp counselors. After twenty-five years, we can still give each other a chuckle by imitating the privileged kids bleating (through the nose, of course), "This is so *boring!*" (These kids would have yawned at the parting of the Red Sea.) The counselors, with no exceptions, have pleasant memories of the poor kids.

In a way, the wealthy children were a sad bunch. They looked better than the less fortunate, yes, but they certainly didn't seem pleased with life. They tired so easily of all we did to entertain them, I shudder to think how they must have vexed their parents. On the other hand, hadn't the doting parents helped bring this situation about? The parents practiced "gilded neglect"—heaping up material things for the kids while giving no thought to the kids' spiritual and moral growth.

I have no doubt that the poor kids enjoyed their week at camp much more than the spoiled ones did. Even with the chiggers, camp was, so one child told me, a "real blast." And with appreciative kids, it was even a "real blast" for the counselors as well.

———

Resolution: Think of some very low-cost, "low-tech" pleasures you have experienced in life. How did these compare with high-cost, "high-tech" pleasures?

56

Elevated Compassion

Open your mouth for the mute,
for the rights of all who are destitute.
Open your mouth, judge righteously,
defend the rights of the poor and needy.

Proverbs 31:8–9

RIDING the "El," Chicago's train system, is an interesting experience. Some of the trains pass through tenement projects that typify the worst type of urban squalor. After riding the trains a few times, I realized that most passengers simply ignored the urban blight altogether. They became conditioned to the ugliness and apparently forgot that such deplorable conditions affected human lives. They read their magazines, napped, worked crossword puzzles, tuned in to their portable stereos, or otherwise distracted themselves from the less-than-scenic scenery.

I sometimes found myself thinking, *Someone should do something.* I realize now that my sympathy must not have run very deep. It is always easy to hope and pray that the government, a charity, a wealthy retired person—always someone *else*—will remedy the situation.

Happily, history is full of examples of people who, empowered by God's Spirit, refused to wait for "someone" to act. The Belgian priest Father Damien heard of the plight of lepers in nineteenth-century Hawaii. Acting as doctor, builder, and superintendent as well as pastor, he formed the lepers into a well-ordered community marked by compassion. Damien himself eventually succumbed to leprosy, but he continued to serve the lepers until his death. Damien understood that a follower of Christ leads a life of loving concern for the downtrodden and forgotten.

Until his death in 1982, Frank Ferree (who was twice nominated for the Nobel Peace Prize) dedicated himself to Volunteer Border Relief, an organization providing poor Mexican immigrants with shelter and medical care. To the very end of his life he tarried among the people, insisting that we cannot bless the poor unless we walk among them as Christ walked.

Speaking of the Nobel Peace Prize, we all remember one of its most appealing winners, Mother Teresa of India. This woman and her many compassionate helpers caught the world's attention, which gives us hope that in this selfish world some people still respect human kindness. Many people forget that in her younger days, Mother Teresa taught at a school for upper-class girls in India. But after two decades she felt God calling her to a greater task: aiding the destitute all around her. She founded her Order of the Missionaries of Charity, whose work continues worldwide.

Father Damien, Frank Ferree, Mother Teresa, and countless other faithful proved that "otherworldly" Christians can make a huge difference in this world through their compassion. It is only the otherworldly who know how to cope with this world.

———

Resolution: Use a Bible concordance to direct you to all the Bible's references to "poor" and "poverty." How many are there? Were you even aware of the importance the Bible places on showing compassion to the poor?

57

Holy Deerslayer

In the path of righteousness is life,
and in its pathway there is no death.

Proverbs 12:28

As I mentioned in the introduction, some say the Book of Proverbs is "short on theology." That isn't quite true. The book's writers mention God many times, and they present him as the just and righteous Judge of man's conduct. Even in passages that do not mention him by name, he is there, looking over man's shoulder, the Observer of all human words and deeds.

As in all other books of the Bible, he is *holy*. Encountering the holy God can be intimidating. When the prophet Isaiah saw the Lord in the temple, his response was "Woe is me!" (Isa. 6:5) There he was, a sinful human being living in a sinful society, and he caught a glimpse of the pure and righteous God. Holiness and righteousness are, to use a term that has lost its original meaning, *awesome*.

Righteousness can indeed be daunting, as is evident in one of the classic American novels, James Fenimore Cooper's *The Deerslayer*. Its title character is a young colonial frontiersman whose moral fiber is often disconcerting to those who meet him. One character says, "I more dread Deerslayer's truth than any enemy! One cannot tamper with such truth—so much honesty—such obstinate uprightness!" If mere human beings can be so unsettling, how much more so the Ruler of the cosmos?

But this powerful, wholly righteous Being is not "out there" somewhere on some distant heavenly throne. He is "down here," not only watching our everyday acts of kindness (and malice), but guiding us to the right, if we so allow. The Book of Proverbs is a kind of balance to books such as Exodus and Leviticus, with their emphasis on the right way to worship God. Worship is important, of course, but Proverbs reminds us that every hour of every day, our deeds, great and small, matter to the God we worship. Proverbs is also a balance to such books as Psalms and Isaiah, with their long poetic passages that inspire us. Those books are wonderful and should be read, but too easily our devotional life can become fixated on lovely and majestic words—not only the books of the Bible, but popular devotional books as well. "Pretty writing" is fine, except that people may admire the words and neglect the message.

So, you see, Proverbs is not "short on theology" at all. It is "everyday theology" that anyone can grasp. And that everyday theology is summed up beautifully in 12:28: If we seek life, not death, we follow righteousness.

———

Resolution: Start your day with a promise to do everything, even the smallest thing, for the glory of God.

58

Sunday Observation

Of what use is money in the hand of a fool,
since he has no desire to get wisdom?

Proverbs 17:16 (NIV)

ONE of the most colorful Christians who ever lived was Billy Sunday (1862–1935), the pro baseball player who became one of the best-known evangelists of his day. Sunday had a homespun directness in his sermons, and he is still widely quoted. One of his many observations: "The fellow that has no money is poor. The fellow that has nothing but money is poorer still."

One wonders how the many rich folk who longed to meet the famous Mr. Sunday received that remark. Were any of them aware that they had "nothing but money"? Probably not. The wealthy usually possess so many "toys" that they can easily distract themselves from their spiritual emptiness.

The wealthiest person I ever knew personally was also the most spiritually empty. He owned rich farmland, worked it hard, and made it produce abundantly. He was a self-made man. He spent little, and he and his overworked wife lived in a modest home, never taking vacations, never spending money on luxuries nor even on items many middle-class people would consider necessities.

It would please me to tell you that instead of spending lavishly on himself, he gave bountifully to charities. He did no such thing. He despised the poor, including his poorer relatives (and all his relatives were poorer than he). He had no children, and his will left the money not to impoverished family members, not to worthy causes, but to . . . rich people. They were not close friends (he had none of those) but merely passing acquaintances. I assume his logic worked something like this: *only people who have money deserve it.* I suspect his sole pleasure in living was knowing that he could keep his money from falling into the hands of people who did not merit it.

"Of what use is money in the hand of a fool?" asks Proverbs. No use whatever. This rich fool loved his money, hoarded it, and never sought to use it wisely or compassionately. We can only hope and pray that the heirs of his huge estate will eventually put his money to some good use.

Certainly this rich man did not take it to his final destination. Contrary to what he thought, and to what most people believed, he died in poverty. In fact, he was probably the poorest human being—in Billy Sunday's terms—I have ever known. Never in his life was he hungry, and yet he died quite empty.

Proverbs 17:16 applies to all people, not just the rich. Any of us, whatever our economic status, can be a "fool" with money. Poor people or middle-class people who win a lottery or suddenly inherit money have been known to squander it and wind up poorer than before. People waste what they have or, like the rich man described above, simply hoard it. Either way they prove the uselessness of money in the hands of the fool. In a world where money could be put to so many noble uses, this is a tragedy. The world, materialistic and godless, asks, "What does a man own?" But God asks, "How does he use it?"

Resolution: Pray for the wealthy, that they use their money and connections to do some good in the world.

59

Hatred Stew

A man's own folly ruins his life,
yet his heart rages against the LORD.

Proverbs 19:3 (NIV)

ADOLF Hitler is one of the most important men in the last century. Yes, he was monstrously evil, but important nonetheless. You can't understand the last hundred years unless you know something about him. For example, people should know that this world-shaking fiend was motivated by hatred and self-pity. Many people (and nations) today feel those same emotions, which is why Hitler's book *Mein Kampf* has become popular reading in certain circles.

When Hitler wrote *Mein Kampf* ("my struggle") in 1923, he was in prison for being a revolutionary agitator. At that time everyone thought he was a failure—as did he. Stewing in his bitterness, he wondered why. Obviously it was not *his* fault—after all, he was (so he believed) a worthy and brilliant man. So his failure must be someone else's fault. Whose? Everyone's—the whole human race's, in fact, except for the Germans, who were good and superior. No one expected in 1923 that this bitter, hate-filled, self-pitying creature would have the power to commit mass murder.

In our own day, Hitler's *Mein Kampf* inspires others who see themselves as failures—either as nations or individuals. Like Hitler in prison, they are angry at God, or fate. But since they cannot fight or injure God, they redirect their hatred against certain groups or nations: America is "the Great Satan," or Israel is. If the Arabs' standard of living is low, it can't be *their* fault. It must be someone else's. Keep these things in mind as the supposedly wise folk of the media puzzle over the "why" of terrorism. It isn't all that complicated. Combine hate and self-pity and you have the makings for horror.

Proverbs 19:3 applies to Hitler, to terrorists, and on a more ordinary level, to the many frustrated, bitter people who make a mess of their own lives but flatly refuse to blame themselves. Substance-abuse treatment centers and psychiatric wards overflow with people who would never dream of accepting responsibility for their wasted lives. The fault lies with . . . whom? God, parents, "the system," whatever. Obviously such people will never find inner peace until they size up their situations and pin the blame for their failures on themselves.

Proverbs 19:3, like the whole Bible, is pro-responsibility. The basic message: if you wonder why your life is not all you had hoped for, consider the possibility that you are responsible before you go searching for scapegoats.

––––––––

Resolution: Get into the "me first" habit when something bad happens to you. Before raging against someone or something else, ask yourself, "Did I myself do anything to bring this about?" If the answer is yes, do the obvious thing—change your behavior.

60

Snapshots from an Album of Saints

The fruit of the righteous is a tree of life,
and whoever captures souls is wise.

Proverbs 11:30

WHAT do saints do in the world? Pray, smile pleasantly, and speak softly? Yes, but they do much more than that. Consider a few "snapshots" from an "album of saints."

Picture 1, America in the 1990s: the Arthur DeMoss Foundation sponsored the "Life—what a beautiful choice" ads you probably saw on TV. Christian businessman Arthur DeMoss, who died a few years ago, left money to support pro-life advertising. The ads were not explicitly Christian, nor even explicitly antiabortion. They simply conveyed, in a nonthreatening, nonjudgmental fashion, the message that with every problem pregnancy, bearing the child is a valid option.

Picture 2, England in the 1840s: the YMCA began, not as a place to learn swimming and lifesaving, but as a place where young men, confronted for the first time with urban immorality, could find wholesome fellowship. The founder, George Williams (1821–1905), was himself a farm lad. Taking a job in London, he was appalled at the drop in morals that occurred in rural men when they came to the city. In 1844 he and other Christian men from various denominations formed the Young Men's Christian Association. The group emphasized prayer, Bible study, and "mental culture." (Physical development was added later.) The Y committed itself to "Jesus Christ as Lord and Savior," and as it expanded into other countries, it provided many young men a wholesome home away from home.

Picture 3, Africa in the 1860s: David Livingstone, the famous Scottish missionary, was even more well known as the first white man to see many parts of Africa. Livingstone's goal was, he said, "Christ and commerce." No, he didn't identify Christianity with capitalism. Rather, in his deep love for Africa and its people, he wanted the horrid slave trade abolished forever. The way to end it was to make Christians of the Africans and to offer the traders economic alternatives to the flourishing slave trade.

Picture 4, England in the 1830s: Christians in high places, notably the politicians Michael Sadler and Lord Shaftesbury, were appalled at the working conditions in industrial England. Many children worked thirteen to sixteen hours per day, and their overseers whipped them if they slacked. Sadler, Shaftesbury, and others gathered facts on the evils of factories and mines and presented them to Parliament. Shaftesbury succeeded in getting his Ten-Hour Act passed in 1847, limiting women and children to ten-hour workdays. Shaftesbury was famous for his statement that "what is morally right can never be politically wrong."

Never heard of these people and their works of compassion? Perhaps not. They were active in "capturing souls," as the verse from Proverbs says. If they go unmentioned in the history books today, surely God has not forgotten their labors. Nor should we. We should work and pray for more of what Proverbs 11:30 calls the "fruit of the righteous."

———

Resolution: Check out a good one-volume survey of Christian history. Pay special attention to people who devoted their lives to works of compassion.

61

Mud and Monsters

*Like a muddied spring or a polluted fountain
is a righteous man who gives way before the wicked.*

Proverbs 25:26

O NE rotten apple spoils the bunch," says the old proverb. It is also true that a rotten bunch will spoil one good apple, very quickly, and with malicious pleasure.

Years ago I taught a fourth-grade Sunday school class. They were all boys, and all friends, and all bad (with one exception). I wish I could sugarcoat this story and say they were "high-spirited," "impish," or "mischievous." But they weren't. They were genuinely mean, nasty kids, and they took pleasure in vexing adults, including the Sunday school teachers they wore out over the years. Many people in the church wondered why my hair did not turn gray, and so did I.

But among these weeds was one lovely flower, a boy who was (no sugarcoating here, just truth) adorable and of course, ill at ease among the others. Within three months of my teaching the class, the good kid had "crossed over." To my dismay, and his parents' as well, he behaved as badly as the others. This, more than anything else, led me to give up the class. The bad kids had tried to break me, and they succeeded. And they had managed to corrupt the one good kid, my only bright spot in teaching the group. Peer pressure is a powerful force, and so is evil, even among children.

About this time I saw the movie *Dangerous Liaisons*, the sordid tale of two bored aristocrats, a man and a woman, who make a game of seducing the innocent. The man delights in cajoling the purest young women into his bed. The woman delights in getting naive young men to fall in love with her, though love is the last thing on her mind. Rather oddly for Hollywood, the movie presented the two seducers not as admirable people but as reptiles. Instead of suggesting they were free-spirited, liberated individuals who introduced others to the pleasures of sex, the film showed them to be manipulative, spiteful fiends. The audience seemed pleased that both characters got their comeuppance at the movie's end. You might say it was a kind of horror movie, with two monsters that are finally destroyed. But in a sense it was more frightening than a horror movie, because we know these types of human monsters really do exist.

One of Jesus' parables was about a shepherd who goes in search of a lost sheep and rejoices at finding it. The sheep, Jesus says, represents a lost sinner who repents, and there is "joy in heaven" (Luke 15:7) over his change of heart. Is there sadness in heaven when the wicked corrupt a righteous person? I know there is grief on earth, as I learned in teaching my Sunday school class. Proverbs had it right: seeing a good soul transformed into a bad one is like seeing a beautiful fountain polluted with sewage.

————

Resolution: Think of situations where people have tried to tempt you to bad behavior. If you gave in, were you sad or happy afterward? Did you ever ask God to give you strength in resisting temptations and peer pressure?

62

God the Lender

Whoever trusts in his riches will fall,
but the righteous will flourish like a green leaf.

Proverbs 11:28

As you probably know, John Wesley was the English minister who, in the 1700s, started the movement known as Methodism. At a time when the Church of England's worship was dry and unemotional, Wesley preached on God's love and the need for each individual to turn his heart to the Father. His teachings found their way into his brother Charles's many classic hymns, and Methodism swept the British Isles and the American frontier as well.

Wesley saw something happen among his followers, a curious phenomenon that has been repeated several times through history: a religious revival touches the poor and working classes, who clean up their lives, become hardworking and respectable, then prosperous, and then—in time—less spiritual. It happened among the Methodists, so much so that in his last years old John had to preach often on the right use of money (aiding one's poorer brothers, that is). Some of the Methodists were well-off, and Wesley had to remind them that their wealth was a gift from God.

Sticking with the Bible, Wesley insisted that our wealth is never, strictly speaking, ours—it is God's, and if we acquired it through cleverness and hard work, wasn't it God who gave us the intelligence and drive? To Wesley, people did not "own" money—they only "borrowed" it from God.

Wesley was no hermit, living on bread and water in the desert, and he did not expect other Christians to be. But he did speak out against needless extravagance in dress, food, and lifestyle. Many times he preached on the Last Judgment, asking his listeners: *What if now, this minute, God called you to account? What if he caught you in the act of purchasing—or boasting about—some new luxury you've acquired?*

He preached that people should use their "borrowed" money to aid the less fortunate. "Do you not know that God entrusted you with that money to feed the hungry, clothe the naked, help the stranger, the widow, the fatherless? How can you defraud the Lord by applying it to any other purpose?" he asked.

Does Wesley sound like a tiresome, humorless fellow? He wasn't. He was warm and loving—like God. But he expected people who called themselves Christians to be compassionate and sharing—like God. For, as Proverbs says, it is the righteous who truly flourish, and riches are useless if we do not put them to work in a needy, hurting world.

Resolution: Read a biography of Methodist founder John Wesley, or, if time is short, look him up in an encyclopedia or on the Internet. He was a truly fascinating character, and one with some sane views about the demands of living a life of faith.

63

Weight on the Truth

Differing weights and differing measures—
the LORD detests them both.

Proverbs 20:10 (NIV)

THE Book of Proverbs often repeats itself—and we can assume that the duplicate points are ones the authors wanted to emphasize. This is true for 20:10, which reiterates the fact that God wants us to be honest in our business dealings. That means, of course, don't cheat your customers or employees.

But an even subtler area of dishonesty is the clock. When an employer pays by the hour, it is obviously theft for an employee to take pay for time when he did no work. To stop fifteen minutes early, to start ten minutes late, to let break time drag on into an hour-long discussion, is to take money under false pretenses.

The fact that the world does this is immaterial. It is still sin—and one in which Christians participate. I was pained for years at watching a woman—regarded as a model believer by our fellow employees—constantly arriving late, leaving early, doing personal work on company time, and "forgetting" to write down vacation and sick days on her time card. Having the office next to hers, I was the only person aware of what she was doing, yet I never reported it because I knew no one would believe me. When I once confronted her privately with the matter, she curtly told me it was no business of mine. Sadly, the company we worked for was a Christian organization.

Spiritual dishonesty may be the most common of all, perhaps because it is the type people are least likely to catch us in. It is so easy to blithely tell a friend we will pray for her, knowing that half an hour later we will have even forgotten the problem she shared. How would she ever know? How easy it is to state we have read such-and-such Christian book, when in fact we never opened the cover. Who would know, and what difference does it make if our friends think us more devout than we really are?

Spiritual honesty is rare, but most desirable. It is the attitude of mind that is open to God. It is the essence of "walking in the light" (1 John 1:7). The spiritually honest person is frank, even about his shortcomings. He has a mind open to God's Spirit, a heart that, while not perfect, does not mind God's searchlight shining into it. The spiritually honest person is willing to see himself as God sees him. Poet Robert Burns wrote of how wonderful it might be if we had the power to see ourselves as others see us. How much more important for the Christian to view himself as God does. How painful, yet how rewarding, to be absolutely honest with God about ourselves.

Resolution: Pray for total honesty in your daily life—at home, at work, everywhere.

64

Give Till It Feels Good

*Whoever is generous to the poor lends to the LORD,
and he will repay him for his deed.*

Proverbs 19:17

DID you know that hospitals were originally "faith homes"? The "hospitals" of the Middle Ages developed from *xenodochia*, inns set up for Christians (many of them poor) on pilgrimages. In time they evolved into hospitals for ailing persons, particularly the indigent. Emperor Charlemagne, impressed by the hospitals' benevolence, decreed that every cathedral and abbey should have a hospital for soothing the sick, lepers, the blind, invalids, orphans, and pilgrims. The abbeys' farms provided food and medicinal herbs. Clothing was distributed, usually at Christmas and Easter.

Medical science was at a primitive stage in the Middle Ages, and generally, hospitals could not *cure* illnesses. But they did provide food, shelter, quiet, cleanliness, a sense of order, and spiritual comfort to the dying. (Obviously such places were the forerunners of hospices today.)

Interestingly, most of the Catholic saints of medieval times were people renowned for aiding the poor. (Catherine of Genoa, who ministered to lepers in the 1400s, was just one example.) Although people associate medieval Christianity with the horrors of the Crusades and the Inquisition, the church chose the benefactors of the downtrodden as its saints, its role models.

Where the Protestant Reformation gained ground in the 1500s, monasteries were closed, and so were the charities they ran. The Reformers have been unfairly accused of not caring for the poor. In fact, Martin Luther, John Calvin, and other Protestant pioneers preached frequently about giving generously. Luther's wife, Katie, sometimes complained that Martin's generosity to poor students, travelers, and religious refugees threatened to empty the family account. Luther claimed that a Christian needed three things converted: heart, mind, and purse.

Luther's Wittenberg Church Order of 1522 established a "common chest" for welfare work. The chest provided interest-free loans to craftsmen and food, clothes, and vocational training for children of the poor, and aided impoverished maidens needing dowries for marriage.

In this era, the idea of permanent poverty gave way to the idea of progress, of upward mobility. This was in keeping with the new possibilities in a society of merchants, where one did not have to inherit wealth to be successful. With effort and business sense, one could advance. The world awakened to this reality, and so did the church. *We must aid the poor*, the Reformers said, *but when possible, we should enable them to raise themselves* (via education and training) *out of poverty.*

Obviously we are heirs of the Reformation, believing we should not only aid the poor but teach and train them to aid themselves. One problem today is that we neglect our obligation. We believe (correctly) that a huge chunk of the taxes we pay goes to welfare programs. It does, but the Bible's words remain: we should *personally* show active compassion for the poor.

———

Resolution: Reach out in person to someone who is poor. Buy him a meal, or an article of clothing, or both.

65

Self-Reliant Saints?

In his heart a man plans his course,
but the LORD determines his steps.

Proverbs 16:9 (NIV)

N OT long ago I visited with my cousin and his children. I asked the eight-year-old son, "Do you pray to God every day?" He replied, "Yes, every night before going to bed."

Then I asked, "Do you pray in the morning?" The reply: "No. During the day I can take care of myself."

My next question was, "Do you get into much trouble when you are asleep?"

"No."

"What about daytime?"

"Sometimes."

My cousin, realizing what I was about, said, "Son, I think it's more important to pray at the beginning of each day. We always need God, especially when we are awake and prone to sin."

A few days later I ran into a young couple I knew from college. Brian was doing well in business, and Rene was somehow managing to raise two small children at home while earning top pay as a freelance artist. They were happy, it seemed, and prosperous. But I could tell something had changed. They weren't the same couple I'd known. God had been left out of their lives. They no longer prayed or read the Bible. Church attendance had dwindled to Easter and Christmas.

They hadn't stopped believing in God. They still wanted, they said, a Christian upbringing for the children. They simply no longer felt the need for God in everyday life. They had lost any sense of dependence on him.

Many years ago Jesus told a story of a rich farmer with fertile land that produced bumper crops. His barns and silos were crammed full. In his prosperity he had no room for God in his life. He was a successful rural capitalist, looking forward to a life of luxury and leisure. Then God spoke words of destiny and terror: "Man, you are a fool. Tonight you will die. You can take nothing with you. You are bankrupt toward me" (see Luke 12:16–21).

The tragedy of the lost world is its lack of need for God. Apart from emergencies, people feel self-sufficient. There are no atheists in foxholes, but what are our needs when we are out of the foxhole?

It is particularly sad to see Christians forgetting their helplessness and ignoring God's offer of daily help. I once met a man, a Christian, who claimed that for the last six months he had lived without any sense of conscious sin in his life. He was rejoicing in his experience of perfection. I shyly commented that his spiritual condition might not be as secure as he thought. I mentioned 1 John 1:8, which tells us that we deceive ourselves if we say we have no sin. My friend assured me that he was, indeed, on the right road. So, I wondered, what need did he have for a Savior?

"A man plans his course, but the Lord determines his steps," says the Proverb. There is no place in Proverbs, or the Bible, or the

Christian life, for someone who believes himself to be totally self-reliant.

————

Resolution: Make a point of stopping some time in the middle of your busy day and asking for God's help, no matter what you are doing.

66

Clay for the Glory of God

Give me neither poverty nor riches;
feed me with the food that is needful for me.

Proverbs 30:8

In Gary's pottery workshop hangs a large plaque with these words: "Whether you eat or drink or whatever you do, do it all for the glory of God." 1 Corinthians 10:31 (NIV).

"I truly believe that," Gary says, "and I think I make pots and bowls and vases for the glory of God." Gary is becoming a rarity in the American economy: a person who actually produces an item with his own hands. "It's genuinely satisfying. I've lived in this area a long time and I have steady customers. But I hold myself to a higher standard than they do. Sometimes I produce a piece with a minor flaw that no customer would spot. It would be easy to place that in the display and sell it. But the right thing to do is throw it on the scrap heap and start a new piece. I won't sell shoddy work."

Pottery is Gary's second career. His first, which he abandoned, paid more: he was an IRS auditor. "I was good at what I did, and the job was perfectly legal. We caught some flagrant tax cheats. But the sad thing was, I felt we were going after harmless, innocent, law-abiding people. I don't think God wants us to do work that is detrimental to humanity. So I dropped out. My pay is much, much less. But I have no regrets."

Gary is delightful to behold: a man who finds fulfillment in his work. I asked him what advice he had for people who don't feel that same contentment. "Part of the problem is training ourselves to look at any task as something God ordained for us to do. I enjoy making a pot out of a lump of shapeless clay. Some people would find that tiresome and boring, others wouldn't. But I firmly believe that we ought to try to please God—and please ourselves in the process—by doing well at whatever we do."

Gary has in his workshop a *Far Side* cartoon of a man in hell, joyfully whistling while being forced to push a wheelbarrow. One of the devils supervising him says to another devil, "You know, we're just not reaching this guy." The cartoon makes an excellent point: work is oppressive only if we think it is. The awareness that God is the ultimate Boss we must please can transform any job.

The apostle Paul spoke of contentment as a good thing (1 Timothy 6:6–8). He was echoing Proverbs 30:8, a prayer for "neither poverty nor riches," but only for "the food that is needful." Gary and other Christians have learned such contentment, no matter what sort of jobs they work.

Resolution: Pray for contentment in your life, being satisfied with the things you possess now.

67

Lunches with Losers

It is better to be of a lowly spirit with the poor than to divide the spoil with the proud.

Proverbs 16:19

ONE thing the Bible is clear about: God doesn't view people the same way we do. People who are "great" by worldly standards may not be so worthy by heavenly standards—and vice versa. Jesus himself had a deep and abiding compassion for "losers": beggars, lepers, the handicapped, society's outcasts.

I volunteered for several months at a downtown church that served inexpensive lunches following a Wednesday noontime worship service. There, in the midst of munching corporation brass, penny-pinching clerical workers, and hungry shoppers, were the biggest "losers" in the city—street people. Their faces were lined with years of worry, work (when it was to be found), sorrows (including being abandoned by their children), and too many life obstacles to enumerate.

These people were old, mostly men. Our youth-obsessed society places them in a special category: people who no longer *do* but only *receive.* They receive Social Security, Medicare, senior discounts, special seating on the bus. Some of them seem to be going through a second childhood, almost completely dependent on others. Those who could not pay for their Wednesday meals often ate at the expense of the church or some compassionate lunchers. These men had nothing useful to contribute at all, except their mere presence.

I had worked for several weeks with the Wednesday lunch crew before I became brave enough to join some of the older men for the meal. Previously I had excused myself to eat in the kitchen, claiming that "the help" had no business eating with the guests. I can be honest enough now to admit that, much as I wanted to follow Jesus' example in mingling with society's cast-off people, I did not want to mingle *too* closely with them.

The meals I shared with those men taught me much about how unimportant "winning" and "losing" (by this world's standards) are. These down-and-out folks appreciated the smallest things in life: a meal simply but thoughtfully prepared, a quiet and unhurried conversation, a shelter from a cold midday downpour, a kind word from a loving pastor.

One of the old men, stoop-shouldered, grizzled Henry, explained his usefulness one Wednesday over a plate of spaghetti and home-baked bread. "Well, son, you know we're s'posed to be actin' like Jesus. Now, mind, I don't heal and I don't preach, and I can't hush up no storms. But I do wander around to a lot of places, and I talk to a good many folks. And I don't own much of anything 'cept the clothes I got on. And I try to say a good word about the Lord whenever I can." Was Henry a "loser"? No way.

Resolution: Offer a kind word—and perhaps a meal—to someone who is a "loser" by this world's standards.

68

Courting God

*It is not good to be partial to the wicked
or to deprive the innocent of justice.*

Proverbs 18:5

*J*UDGMENTAL is a favorite smear word today. No one wishes to be
called "judgmental," and so the Bible's notion of God as a heavenly Judge is extremely unpopular. This wasn't so in times past. One
of the great masterpieces of world art is Michelangelo's stunning (and
frightening) painting of the Last Judgment on a wall of the Vatican's
Sistine Chapel. Michelangelo's is only one of thousands of such paint-
ings. Apparently earlier generations of believers took some pleasure
and comfort in images of justice being done at the end of time—the
righteous going to heaven, the wicked going to hell. We can assume
that part of the pleasure was the painful awareness that in this world
the wicked often go unpunished while the innocent suffer.

Not many artists today are painting the Last Judgment. Today's
God is loving, caring, good . . . but not judgmental. People today, including many Christians, are uncomfortable with Bible passages that
call upon God to "judge the nations."

Author C. S. Lewis understood this. In his *Reflections on the Psalms*,

Lewis claimed that part of our problem with thinking of God as Judge is that we imagine a *criminal* court, while the Bible presents judgment more in terms of a *civil* action. People in the Bible looked to God as the fair-minded (and final) Judge who would hear the pleas of the "little people" whom the privileged oppressed and exploited. This Judge would make the defendants "pay damages"—if not in this world, then in the next. So throughout the Bible we see God described as the Judge who will "forget not the complaint of the poor," the one who "renders true judgment" and "helps all the meek upon earth." God, unlike earthly judges, cannot be bribed, nor is he swayed by someone's wealth or social status.

Proverbs 18:5 is directed not at God, of course, but at earthly judges. In effect, the verse tells them to be like God—take the side of the innocent against the wicked. Be fair. Take no bribes and do not be partial to the wealthy and powerful.

Will that ever happen in this fallen world? Not in every case, certainly. The rich can, as some notorious trials showed us in recent years, literally get away with murder. The law is usually on the side of those with money and prestige, and the system too seldom benefits those without. But the Bible is clear that judges, like everyone else, will have to face the Last Judgment.

———

Resolution: Think of people you know who have been involved in civil lawsuits. Were they given justice in court? Did they think the judges were fair?

69

Kings and Minimum Wage Earners

Do you see a man skillful in his work?
He will stand before kings.

Proverbs 22:29

Is it really true, as Martin Luther said, that "a dairymaid can milk cows for the glory of God"? How do the Christian butcher, baker, hamburger-flipper, and software engineer honor God on their jobs?

Randy is working, for the time being, cleaning at a fast-food restaurant. Like many graduates with liberal arts degrees, he didn't find a cozy salaried position the day he graduated from college. In fact, he's been "brooming Wendy's," as he puts it, since right after graduation—eighteen months ago. Randy's situation is a familiar one today: he is working a job that is beneath his training and his mental abilities.

"The biggest temptation is to fall into bitterness and frustration," Randy told me. "One of my college roommates became an alcoholic. He can't find a job better than working part-time at a copy center.

The system just hasn't found a place for him yet. It would be so easy to fall into the same trap he has."

How does an underemployed, *magna cum laude* graduate from a respected college "work for the Lord"? Randy explains: "Even though there are lots of people around me while I work, it's actually pretty solitary—the broom, the Lord, and me. Before I start my workday, I pray. I ask God to keep me from bitterness and anger. I still pray that I'll find a job that matches my academic qualifications."

And in the meantime? "If you've ever eaten in a place that's dirty or untidy, you know how important cleanliness is. I'm not using my college smarts when I sweep and mop, but I try to concentrate on doing the job I'm hired for: making the place sparkle."

I asked Randy if he reaps any rewards from his efforts. "Oftentimes, none at all. Once in a blue moon some customer will compliment me on how the place looks. But our manager hardly mentions it. He seems pleased that he pays me the same as the high school kids and I work harder than they do. In fact, some of the kids ask me why I knock myself out.

"But I gain nothing from being frustrated or bitter. I gain a lot from knowing that people who breeze in here for a quick meal enjoy their time more if the place is spotless. They may never thank me, but I know it pleases God."

Many people share Randy's situation: working for less pay and fewer prospects than their training prepared them for. But all of them can, like Randy, strive for excellence even if their daily grind seems truly grinding.

I asked Randy if he expected to "stand before kings," as Proverbs says. He replied that he expects God to give him another and better job somewhere down the line. And he expects to stand before the King—the only king who matters—at some future date, and I expect he will not be ashamed of his work at that time.

Resolution: Talk to Christians you know who work hard at their jobs. What motivates them? Are they ever bitter or frustrated? How do they cope?

70

Blessed Are the Poor Aiding the Poor

*Whoever closes his ear to the cry of the poor
will himself call out and not be answered.*

Proverbs 21:13

SHOULDN'T people of faith reach out to the poor? According to the Bible, yes. And according to history, they always have. But in the late 1800s, new ideas were making headway in the world—and the church. Charles Darwin's teachings on evolution affected social thinkers. "Social Darwinism" and the notion of "survival of the fittest" became popular. For many people, the ideas meant that the poor were the "unfit," who would not (in the natural order of things) survive. This is far from biblical, but it had its effect on people's attitudes toward charity.

Self-made millionaires like Andrew Carnegie had doubts about traditional charity. They thought that libraries, museums, and city parklands would "ennoble" the poor and make them strive for a higher life; so the millionaires (many of them claiming to be Christian) launched an age of "architectural charity." It was all impressive, but not helpful for the poor. It was the modern equivalent of medieval lords giving money to build magnificent cathedrals—in fact, this was the great age in the U.S. of wealthy Christians donating enormous sums for splendid churches.

But there was more going on then than building splendid churches for the wealthy. The late 1800s was also the time of "laymen's societies," clubs of Christian businessmen who, having succeeded in life, wanted to practice both evangelism and social service. The Presbyterian Brotherhood in Chicago was one of many lay-led men's associations that stressed a *practical* Christianity. The men put their business shrewdness to good use in setting up employment networks for the urban poor. The lay brotherhoods also encouraged businessmen to pay fair wages and develop safe working environments.

In our own day, many churches manage to combine evangelism with active compassion for the poor. Notably in Latin America, Pentecostal churches reach out especially to the indigent. Some of their storefront churches look shabby, yet many are *growing* rapidly—the Pentecostal explosion is nothing short of phenomenal.

Here is a recurring feature of Christian aid to the poor: many poorer Christians give generously. In the U.S. today, for example, small denominations with names like Allegheny Wesleyan Methodist Connection show high levels of giving, even though their members rank low on the economic scale. Christians in small denominations or "house churches" often feel a spiritual solidarity. With little to give, they give much. This was also the pattern with the earliest persecuted Christians, such as the original Quakers and Methodists.

This connectedness is often missing in our mobile society, where our cars allow us to drive to a church with people of our own class.

Generally, the more separated we are from the poor, physically and emotionally, the less likely we are to help.

Resolution: If you can, set aside the cost of one of your meals each week and donate it to the poor.

71

He Slash, She Slash

He who guards his lips guards his life,
but he who speaks rashly will come to ruin.

Proverbs 13:3 (NIV)

ONE of the most poignant stories in the Bible is that of King David and his dramatic falling-out with his wife Michal. It is particularly touching because we learn early in their story that Michal loved David intensely, and that she, daughter of King Saul, went to great lengths to protect her husband from her father (1 Sam. 18–19). Her love and loyalty should have made for a happy marriage (if we can overlook the fact that the kings of Israel had more than one wife—a situation most of us would consider less than ideal). Yet in 2 Samuel 6 we read of a mutual tongue-lashing that soured the relationship permanently.

David had literally danced in the streets when the ark of the covenant was brought into Jerusalem. The Bible tells us he was wearing an ephod—meaning, probably, a sort of loincloth, which would be the equivalent of a man today dancing in the streets in gym shorts or boxers. Michal, a king's daughter as well as a king's wife, found David's behavior disgusting.

Michal daughter of Saul watched from a window. And when she saw King David leaping and dancing before the LORD, she despised him in her heart.

. . . When David returned home to bless his household, Michal daughter of Saul came out to meet him and said, "How the king of Israel has distinguished himself today, disrobing in the sight of the slave girls of his servants as any vulgar fellow would!" (2 Sam. 6:16, 20 NIV)

Here was her husband on an emotional high, gleeful that the ark (the symbol of God's presence) was now in his nation's capital. Instead of rejoicing with him, or saying nothing at all, Michal belittled. *You've made a fool of yourself, King, acting like a commoner.* We can almost imagine a hiss in her voice, a look of undisguised contempt on her face. (On the other hand, she might have looked cool and disdainful, which is no better.) So, you're feeling good, are you, David? Well, you look like a perfect buffoon.

She had meant to cut him deeply, and she had succeeded. David threw belittlement right back at her. "David said to Michal, 'It was before the LORD, who chose me rather than your father or anyone from his house when he appointed me ruler over the LORD's people Israel—I will celebrate before the LORD'" (v. 21). He went for a vulnerable spot: God had abandoned her father as king, preferring David instead. Michal, putting down her husband, implied that a truly dignified king (like her father, no doubt) would not have danced half-naked in the streets.

The story has, not surprisingly, an unpleasant ending: "Michal daughter of Saul had no children to the day of her death" (v. 23). Some commentators interpret this to mean that God punished Michal with barrenness. More likely there is a more obvious meaning: she and David never had relations again after this hostile encounter. Wife mocks husband while he is at the height of religious ecstasy. Husband insults wife's family. End of relationship.

Both lost the battle. A marriage was ruined because two strong-willed people spoke rashly. Michal and David had both spoken rashly, not "guarded their lips." What might have happened if these two strong-willed people, so good at using words, had used them to build each other up instead of tearing each other down?

———

Resolution: The next time someone offends you with words or be-havior, resolve to keep silent—no matter what.

72

No King But God

Many seek an audience with a ruler,
but it is from the LORD that man gets justice.

Proverbs 29:26 (NIV)

IN the late 1700s, the American colonies made two fateful deci
sions: they declared independence from the kingdom of Great
Britain, and they refused to enthrone a king of their own. Both were
wise choices, the second as important as the first.

George Washington, our first president, made it clear he had no
wish to be made a king. He and the other Founders were wise
enough to understand this truth about kings: when you concentrate
too much power in the hands of one person, you are asking for trouble. A republic with elected officials is not perfect, but it is better
than a monarchy.

The Founders' skepticism about kings was probably rooted in the
Bible. The Bible presents us with dozens of kings, and most of them
are rogues and tyrants—not just the kings of oppressive foreign
powers, but the kings of Israel, God's chosen nation, as well. In 1
Samuel 8 we have the sad story of Israel asking for a king so they
could be "like all the nations" (8:5). The prophet Samuel, Israel's

judge at the time, gave them a stern warning about what to expect from a king. In 8:10–16 Samuel lists the various ways a king will tax the people, draft the men, and, in general, make free people into slaves. His prophecy proves true, and we see in the books of Kings and Chronicles that Israel's kings were a sorry lot. A few saintly ones ruled—Hezekiah and Josiah, for example (2 Kings 18–20, 22–23)—but most were both bad rulers and bad men. It is a cliche, but a true one: power corrupts, which is why most human kings have disappointed the people they rule. Rather than seeking the welfare of their nation and its people (especially its oppressed), they have made themselves rich and favored their own elites. Most have been unscrupulous about eliminating rivals and rebels. Good and moral leaders are the exception, not the rule.

Proverbs 29:26 reflects the Bible's view of kings—and of government in general. The message is simple enough: don't expect too much of your king (or president, or dictator, or legislature). We ought to respect and pray for our government (Rom. 13:1–7, 1 Peter 2:17), but "it is better to take refuge in the Lord than to trust in princes" (Psalm 118:9). Human institutions like courts, legislatures, and all government agencies may at times work for justice and for the general good of society—sometimes, but not often enough. Ultimately, only God can be relied on. "Blessed are the people whose God is the Lord" (Psalm 144:15).

———

Resolution: Pause for a moment and pray for the president, the Congress, the Supreme Court, and your own state's governor and legislature. Pray that they will execute justice and mercy in their work. Then remind yourself that the Christian's ultimate security is God alone.

73

Bruiseless Abuse

The mouth of the righteous brings forth wisdom,
but the perverse tongue will be cut off.

Proverbs 10:31

Here's a loaded question: are men and women the same? Consider what studies of children have found: Around age ten, roughly the same percent of girls as boys are overtly aggressive, given to open confrontation when angered, willing to fight physically. But by age thirteen or so, a noticeable difference between the sexes emerges: girls become more adept than boys at nonviolent tactics—such as ostracism, malicious gossip, and indirect vendettas. Boys, for the most part, simply continue being confrontational when angered. So girls aren't necessarily "nicer" than boys; they simply have other ways of being mean. Fewer cuts and bruises can be attributed to girls, and thus they don't often visit the principal's office. But they can do harm.

So can boys who are less physically aggressive. I speak from personal experience. While I avoided fistfights (since I knew I would probably lose), I tongue-lashed with the best of them, having a deep reservoir of sarcasm at my disposal. When I became editor of the school newspaper, I used my poison pen whenever possible to take slaps at the kids who were popular. I would never have dreamed of fighting in the school yard, and I never ended up in the principal's office, as so many boys did. But my words did some damage, as I fully intended them to do.

Christians, both men and women, are particularly prone to tongue problems. No one would dream of physical violence in church or in a Christian organization, but the words run hot and venomous. While Christians will shun gathering around the water cooler to swap dirty jokes or stories about fellow employees' promiscuity, they will spread rumors, insinuate, artfully sugarcoat sarcasm, use all manner of nonverbal cues to signal that a particular person is "not really one of us," and then they will generally *not* feel guilt for so doing. After all, the verbal sins are invisible (to humans, that is, but not to God). And while the Ten Commandments plainly tell us not to kill, steal, commit adultery, or take God's name in vain, the Big Ten say nothing about doing harm with words . . . or do they?

What about this one: "You shall not give false testimony against your neighbor" (Exod. 20:16 NIV)? Technically, this is talking about lying in court. Much can be at stake in such a situation—perhaps even the person's life. But just as Jesus said that the commandment "Do not commit adultery" entailed more than just avoiding the physical act (Matt. 5:27–28), so we can assume that the ninth commandment applies to more than courtrooms. Taken to its logical conclusion, the commandment requires us to avoid hurting others with our words. Proverbs 10:31 warns that "the perverse tongue will be cut off." Literally? No. But spiritually, yes. The Bible is pretty clear: if we won't control our tongues, we are far from God.

———

Resolution: In your conversations with friends, family members, or fellow workers, try applying this old rule: say nothing about a person that you would not be willing to say if he were present.

74

Hellaciously Proud

The LORD detests all the proud of heart.
Be sure of this: They will not go unpunished.

Proverbs 16:5 (NIV)

SOME people spend their entire lives flying the pennants of their pride. Their vanity is breathtaking. They are legends in their own minds. Somehow they manage to turn all of reality into a plea for themselves. Essentially, such a person is deaf to any voice but his own.

The Bible has a label for pride: it is a *sin*—a big one, in fact. As the authors of the Bible understood it, pride was idolatry: worshiping not the true God, but a false one—the self. But beyond that, self-centered people do tremendous harm in the world. We can trace just about every sin—murder, theft, adultery, lying—to this fundamental belief of the proud person: "*I* am what matters. *I* am the center of the universe. My pleasure and happiness are the only things that really count." The proud person is not an atheist who says, "There is no God" but rather someone who says, "There is no God *but me!*"

Proverbs 16:5 contains a threat: the proud will not go unpunished. Did the author mean in this life, or later? Frankly, we aren't quite sure. But later generations of Jews and Christians understood the verse this way: God will penalize the proud, perhaps in this life, but definitely in the next. The humble people will find eternal bliss in heaven, the proud can spend eternity fondling their own egos in hell. (A proud person couldn't enjoy heaven anyway—how could he endure God being the center of attention, and not himself?)

The subject of hell is not exactly fashionable, not even in the most conservative churches. Perhaps a past generation of preachers overemphasized the subject. The present generation neglects it entirely, which is odd, for the loving, merciful God of the Bible is also a God who hates sin—the same God who gives people the free will to reject his love and compassion and if they wish, spend their entire lives worshiping themselves.

My great-grandfather had grown up listening to sermons on hell. As he aged, he was aware that preachers seldom spoke on the subject. I recall him saying, "When the world got rid of hell, it would regret it only once, and that would be always." I have to agree. Hell is serious because sin is. Of course God is wrathful and threatening, for he sees (more than any of us do, individually) the hurt vain, self-seeking humans cause.

"They will not go unpunished." You don't have to *like* Bible verses such as this. You do have to admit that they exist, and that the Bible's authors saw no contradiction between God the loving Father and God the angry Judge of sin.

———

Resolution: Think of the vainest, most self-centered people you have ever known. Can you imagine them enjoying the fellowship and worship that are heaven?

75

Cut 'Em Down to Size

The words of a gossip are like choice morsels;
they go down to a man's inmost parts.

Proverbs 18:8 (NIV)

INSULTING someone to his face has its hazards. Sometimes he fights back and is a more skilled belittler than we are. But there's no such danger at a distance. This is why we take such pleasure in slurring the famous.

What lies behind our fascination with celebrities? They are bigger than life there on the movie or TV screen, not real, yet somehow more real than people we see every day in person. The moving image intrigues us, just as it did a century ago when motion pictures were new. We're aware that these bigger-than-life people are "glued together" via the magic of makeup, plastic surgery, designer clothes, personal trainers, and whatnot. That fakery does not turn us off—quite the contrary. It is the fact that they are not like us that fascinates us. We are ordinary. They are *extra*ordinary.

The magazines and talk shows present celebrities to us to be adored, and we do so. And yet we're perfectly willing to change our attitude when the unpleasant truth about some celebrity comes to light. Ah, joy! The superhuman turns out to be human after all. In fact, their morals indicate they are less than we are ourselves. The extraordinary is subordinary.

Recall Don Henley's song "Dirty Laundry," a spoof of superficial newscasters, but also a slap in the face of the public, the people who ask for and get "dirty laundry" on the rich and famous. The media and the public collaborate to create the famous, but fame is subject to gravity: what goes up must come down. Once the media airs spicy news, we sneer and click our tongues and say, "Scumbags."

What do we gain from looking down on celebrities? Not a thing—except a boost to our own egos. *I may have a dead-end job, but at least I don't act like that movie star. My marriage isn't so great, but I don't sleep around like that rock star.* Can anyone doubt that the tabloids sell so well because people pump their egos by reading them?

Some would say this is fine—no harm is done, the celebrities themselves probably don't give two hoots about what we say about them. And yet it affects *us*. It narrows the heart and mind, concentrating attention on people we will never meet. It diverts our attention from the real people around us who need our love and concern. Instead of behaving as if we are made in the image of God, we make ourselves into dirt-dishing scandalmongers.

Proverbs 18:8 speaks of gossip as "choice morsels"—that is, *juicy tidbits*. But these tidbits, tasty though they are, go down to "the inmost parts." They do not nourish the soul, but damage it. Sadly, they injure the gossip more than the distant person who is the subject of the gossip.

———

Resolution: If you have formed the habit of following celebrity "news," see if you can skip a day—or week—without tracking such "news." See if this "gossip fast" doesn't improve your spiritual health.

76

Confessional Cruelty

Whoever conceals his transgressions will not prosper,
but he who confesses and forsakes them will obtain mercy.

Proverbs 28:13

"C ONFESSION is good for the soul," so the saying goes. It is good
for the soul of the one who confesses, and for the one who
hears him.

Or is it? I occasionally force myself to watch the television scream-
fests or "embarrassment shows" or "confession orgies" that pass for
entertainment these days. You know the formula: Person X sits on
the stage, confesses a naughty secret to the audience, then to Person
Y, the spouse/mate/parent who had been cloistered backstage. Person X sits there with a half-proud, half-embarrassed smile, while
Person Y screams, weeps, or swears. I have never managed more
than ten minutes of this sort of "entertainment." The Romans who
applauded the gladiators' slaughter were horrible people, and I have
to wonder about addicts of this type of television also. Would it
please them if the quarreling parties literally did rip each other to
shreds in front of the cameras?

What is it that is missing from "confession TV"? Read Proverbs

28:13: "he who confesses and forsakes" his sins obtains mercy. Confessing is part of the process. Forsaking is the other. These TV shows make it clear that confession is easy—even fun and exciting. But forsaking? Renouncing? That might make for interesting—even moral—TV viewing. But with less slugging and profanity, would audiences like it?

Martin Luther summed up the matter nicely: "To do so no more is the truest repentance." A few years back a presidential candidate admitted to a world audience that he had "caused pain in [his] marriage." He *appeared* sorry—then for eight years he proceeded to prove he was not sorry at all, for he went on to cause a great deal more pain. Apparently confession is no longer admitting sin and turning from it but admitting sin and flaunting it—which means the person does not think it is sin at all.

Let's admit that some of the victims on the cruelty-TV shows are not very nice people themselves. At times the programs seem to show us depraved people hurting other depraved people, and we wonder if we should even sympathize. And yet, viewers (myself included) perhaps hold out the hope that, after one of these loud, heated confrontations, the person who confesses will indeed do the moral thing and *repent*. I have not seen it happen, but it would be refreshing, and it would give us all hope that culture has not lost its soul.

———

Resolution: Consider times in your life when you admitted a wrong and even said "I'm sorry"—but didn't stop committing the sin. Consider the flip side: How have you felt when someone admitted they had wronged you, said they were sorry—then showed no sign of stopping the behavior?

77

Sacrificing Morals

*The sacrifice of the wicked is an abomination to the LORD,
but the prayer of the upright is acceptable to him.*

Proverbs 15:8

*To do righteousness and justice
is more acceptable to the LORD than sacrifice.*

Proverbs 21:3

SOMETIME in my childhood I overheard a conversation between two older ladies, who were discussing a widow friend of theirs.

"I heard she met a nice man who is a regular churchgoer."

"That's nice. But is he a *good* man?"

I was too young then to grasp the meaning, though it is perfectly clear now. One lady assumed that "a regular churchgoer" would be a good match for a nice widow. The other lady assumed nothing of the kind. A regular churchgoer was *probably* a good catch—but not necessarily. The lady who asked, "Is he a *good* man?" had enough wisdom and experience to know that not all churchgoers are good people.

These two verses from Proverbs both refer to sacrifice, which is no longer a part of our religious practices. But for "sacrifice" substitute one of these: *church attendance, religious observances,* or *religious activities.* The meanings of 15:8 and 21:3 are the same, yesterday and today: if you go through the motions of religion but your heart isn't right, God is not fooled.

I have heard my grandmother and her generation refer to people who "were there every time the church door opened." They considered this a good thing. But God is more perceptive than we humans are, and surely there are people whose feet enter the church but whose hearts are elsewhere.

These two verses from Proverbs could have been plucked right out of some of the prophets' books, for the prophets showed a keen awareness of religious hypocrisy. Amos saw that God took no delight in man's "solemn assemblies" (5:21) or "the noise of your songs" (5:23)—not so long as the people neglected justice and righteousness. Another prophet, Micah, asked, "What does the LORD require of you / but to do justice, and to love kindness, / and to walk humbly with your God?" (6:8) The prophets would have understood the old lady who asked, "But is he a *good* man?"

Proverbs is a very *practical* book. It is concerned with morality, not with religious ceremonies or worship. In fact, almost the only times its authors mention these are in 15:8 and 21:3, where they make it clear that religion by itself cannot please God. So the person who sings a beautiful solo during Sunday worship may please human ears—but not God's, if that person's heart and behavior are not right. And the eloquent preacher may mesmerize the congregation and even bring people nearer to God—yet God wants righteous living more than beautiful words. The song and the sermon may be offered up as gifts to God, yet the gifts are no better than the givers. Ditto for tithing, chairing a committee, serving as a deacon or elder, teaching a class, working with the poor. Ditto for being there every time the church door opens. All our religious practices mean nothing if our lives don't chime in.

———

Resolution: Think of people you have known who were "religious" but who did not impress you as particularly good or kind people. Then take stock of your own condition. Do you sometimes show more concern for seeming religious than for pleasing God?

78

Sharpening the
Spiritual Fellowship

As iron sharpens iron,
so one man sharpens another.

Proverbs 27:17 (NIV)

BEHOLD, how these Christians love one another." So said a pagan intellectual in the Roman Empire. While his remarks about Christians focused on their moral scruples and their lack of intellectual polish and civic loyalty, the critic had to admit that they were a loving fellowship.

The church, as the New Testament shows, was from the beginning a fellowship based on shared beliefs, morals, and concern for the hurting. As seen in the Book of Acts, the first believers in Jerusalem practiced a kind of communitarianism, voluntarily sharing their property with other believers (Acts 4:32). As the church expanded beyond Jerusalem, believers felt a bond with believers in other locales, as seen in Paul's concern for the churches helping the Jerusalem church.

For believers across the empire, worship was a genuinely *festive* response to having the "vertical" (man and God) relationship made right. They also celebrated each other, the "horizontal" relationships. God was Father, other believers were brothers and sisters, and the early Christians did not toss the terms about thoughtlessly.

These people tangibly expressed love in worship. All believers were privileged to bring offerings—money, wine, fruits, and grain—and these were later distributed to the needy among the believers. Where there was excess, the early church gave it to nonbelievers, a fact that impressed the pagans. They could mock the Christian worship services, but they could not mock charity.

Worship usually included the kiss of peace, which meant that disagreeing brethren had literally to kiss and make up before coming to the Lord's table. The document known as the *Didache*, probably written around A.D. 100, speaks of the early Christians' emphasis on harmony.

Penitence, a primitive-sounding concept to moderns, was one way the body of Christ expressed its oneness. A man's sin was not his own. It was a spot on Christ's body, and everyone was concerned. The fellowship excluded anyone who committed a grave sin until he had shown sincere repentance. When the penitent person's sincerity was evident, the believers received him with great joy. Penitence was medicine, not punishment.

In the Roman Empire's churches, rich and poor, slave and free mingled freely. A former slave became bishop of Rome, proof that wealth and breeding were not essentials to leadership in Christ's church. Wealthy believers were generous in helping orphans and widows, something almost unknown among pagans. It was common practice in some areas to will part of one's estate to "Christ our Lord." This legacy was designated the "alimony of the poor," and was distributed by the church.

Is this all "ancient history"? Not at all. Among many Christians,

Proverbs 27:17 still applies—"iron sharpens iron," meaning that people grow spiritually through their interaction together.

————

Resolution: If you enjoy a loving fellowship with other people of faith, thank God for it. If you don't, seek out such a fellowship.

79

Seaside Vocations

The light of the righteous shines brightly,
but the lamp of the wicked is snuffed out.

Proverbs 13:9 (NIV)

ONE of the world's lesser-known heroines was Josephine Butler (1828–1907). She took on one of the world's chronic evils, the sexual exploitation of women. Butler lived in Victorian England, generally considered the seat of propriety and restraint. But Victorian England had its seamy side. Prostitution ran rampant, particularly in port towns, and there was a thriving business in procuring young girls for the trade. (The age of consent then was only twelve.)

Butler lived in the squalid seaside city of Liverpool, noted for prostitution. She helped establish homes for the women, giving them a chance to pursue another way of life. Then she turned her attention to Britain's Contagious Disease Acts, passed in the 1860s. In theory, the acts aimed to control the spread of venereal disease by requiring the arrest and medical examination of women suspected of infection.

Butler and many other Christians saw the Contagious Disease Acts differently: Britain, a supposedly Christian nation, was choosing to regulate prostitution instead of outlaw it. Men who patronized prostitutes weren't being asked to change their behavior at all, and the Acts only ensured they would get "clean" prostitutes.

Butler organized the Ladies' National Association for Repeal, dedicated to informing the public that the acts failed as health measures and contributed to the exploitation of women. She circulated petitions, debated anyone who cared to confront her, and supported parliamentary candidates who promised to repeal the acts. She was successful: the acts were repealed in 1886. She also campaigned to raise the age of consent to sixteen; again, she was successful. This helped reduce the procurement of young girls as prostitutes.

Josephine Butler is a good example of a faithful person coping with social evil. She worked on the individual-focused street level—establishing homes for destitute women, giving them an alternative to the life of prostitution—but also on the legislative level, working to change laws that encouraged exploitation. In her tireless round of public debates, influencing members of Parliament, and enlisting the aid of sympathetic newspaper editors (the media moguls of their day), she is almost a prototype of twenty-first-century Christians agitating for social change. She didn't stamp out prostitution in Britain, nor did she expect to. But she did diminish the problem, and she chose her methods well.

Josephine Butler also proved Christians need to be "in the trenches"—actually helping the "untouchables" improve their lot. If just one sinner is transformed, then so is society. With each transformation, believers salt and light the world. As C. S. Lewis said, "He who converts his neighbor has performed the most practical Christian-political act of all."

"The light of the righteous shines brightly"—and Josephine Butler is a neglected, but not completely forgotten, heroine of the faith. Who remembers today the flesh-peddlers and exploiters who opposed her moral reforms?

Resolution: Do some inquiring—via friends, your church, the Internet—about people of faith who attack social problems in your area. You might even go a step further and volunteer some of your own time and money to help them.

8o

Vengeance Topsy-Turvy

If your enemy is hungry, give him bread to eat,
and if he is thirsty, give him water to drink,
for you will heap burning coals on his head,
and the LORD *will reward you.*

Proverbs 25:21–22

LOVE your enemies"? Really? Nothing goes against our nature more than this moral mandate. But Jesus commanded us to do so (Matt. 5:44), and as you can see from these verses from Proverbs, Jesus was only reminding people of something already taught in the Old Testament. The idea must have jarred his listeners as much as it jars us today: Give food to a hungry enemy? Isn't that asking a bit much of us?

Of course it is. It raises the bar so extremely high that most of us will shrug our shoulders and say, "Well, a lovely idea, but who can do it?"

Actually, it happens more often than people think. Soldiers, oddly enough, witness it in wartime. If you visited the Fredericksburg National Military Park in Virginia, you would see a statue of the "Angel of Marye's Heights," a Confederate soldier who mercifully carried water to wounded Yankee soldiers after the battle. His compassion made a deep impression not only on the Yankees (who did not fire at him, of course) but on his fellow Confederates as well. The fact that he was known as "the Angel" tells us something: such behavior is rare enough among ordinary humans.

Yet occasions arise for all of us to bless, and therefore "heap burning coals" on our enemies' heads. Years ago I had a next-door neighbor who detested me, and there was always a chilly silence if we happened to be out in our yards at the same time. (We took steps to avoid this, naturally.) As it happened, I saw him one day in a mall parking lot, with the hood of his car raised up. I guessed, correctly, that his battery was dead—and I had jumper cables in my car. Quite honestly I was tempted to drive by him and say something like "I've got jumper cables with me, and if you weren't such a jerk I would help you out." A second option was simply to drive away (I didn't think he had seen me). But I did stop and ask him if he needed help—half-expecting he might swear at me just for speaking to him. It was an awkward moment, but if you have ever been stranded, you know that you inevitably feel grateful to someone who helps you. He did, and said so. Things were not all warm and cuddly afterward, but some of the ice melted.

We can never be sure in such situations that the persons will respond with gratitude. Perhaps they will not, and we will feel foolish. It does hurt to be mocked for showing kindness. But from God's point of view, it is worth the risk. Perhaps the mockers experience their "coals of fire," even if we do not see the burning ourselves. We can only "heap the coals" and hope for the best.

———

Resolution: Think of times you had opportunities to do a good turn to someone you disliked. Did you follow through, or decide they didn't deserve your kindness? If you followed through, were things changed between you afterward?

81

Tolerating Intolerance

The righteous will never be uprooted,
but the wicked will not remain in the land.

Proverbs 10:30 (NIV)

I N recent years, the news media have surprised many people with stories of Christian missionaries suffering persecution. Religious persecution? Really? In this modern, tolerant world of ours? Indeed. Some things never change.

Think back a few hundred years. As European Christians took the faith abroad, an old problem returned: persecution by unbelievers. Missionaries made converts in Japan, but in 1614 the Japanese government issued an edict ordering European Christians to leave, and Japanese Christians to renounce the faith. From 1614 to 1643, at least five thousand Japanese Christians were murdered—some beheaded, some burned at the stake, some killed by "water torture"— having boiling sulphur water slowly poured into slits cut in their flesh. Some were even crucified.

In the 1600s in Europe (where everyone was supposedly a Christian), various groups endured persecution. One was the people who called themselves "Children of Light" or simply "Friends"—they were better known as the "Quakers." Many Quakers were publicly whipped, branded on the forehead (often with a B for "blasphemer"), imprisoned, and even executed.

Consider John Wesley and the original Methodists in the 1700s: Wesley was a Church of England minister, appalled by the spiritual deadness of his church. He and his circuit-riding preachers took to the road, speaking to the masses, insisting that a personal relationship with Christ was essential. Hecklers harassed the early Methodists by throwing stones, rotten eggs, and fruit. They beat some Methodists, tarred and feathered others.

In the twentieth century, a supposedly enlightened and "tolerant" age, intolerance of Christians was the rule. Those who led the Russian Revolution in 1917 set the standard. The new Communist regime aimed to exterminate Christianity and all other religions. In 1925 the government-sponsored League of Militant Godless launched a propaganda war of anti-Christian films, plays, lectures, and museum exhibits. Christians could not evangelize, engage in charitable work or education, or hold Bible study or fellowship meetings. Clergymen were listed as an "exploiting element" and frequently harassed, many of them sent to prison or executed.

The former Soviet Union's anti-Christian tactics (physical abuse coupled with highly organized and efficient propaganda) have been copied and are still used in many nations, notably China, North Korea, Vietnam, Laos, Cuba, Nigeria, Sudan, Saudi Arabia, Uzbekistan, and Egypt. As this list indicates, Communists and extremist Muslims are the worst offenders.

Believers can take comfort in this: God is with his people, and where there is persecution, they must be doing something right. "Blessed are those who are persecuted because of righteousness, / for theirs is the kingdom of heaven" (Matt. 5:10 NIV). In heaven, though not in this world, "the righteous will never be uprooted."

Resolution: Find out if your own Christian fellowship supports any missionaries in other countries. Learn more about the work they do.

82

A Nightingale's Toughness

If you faint in the day of adversity,
your strength is small.

Proverbs 24:10

Do we rely on our own strength, or God's? According to the Bible, the answer is yes—both, that is. If you read the Bible from one end to the other, you will find verses that tell people to rely on God—as well as verses such as Proverbs 24:10 that seem to say, "Put up your dukes, kid!" No contradiction here, and no inconsistency, just the awareness that even the toughest people need a power outside themselves, and that seemingly weak people may be more rugged than they realize.

For a person of faith, perhaps it is not always clear whose strength saw him through a crisis, his own or God's. The many believers who have been persecuted or even martyred for the faith were probably not sure. In a sense all strength comes from God, for it is he who made us. But we are never merely robots powered from the outside source. Toughness is a mental and spiritual quality we can choose to cultivate—or not, as we see in Proverbs 24:10.

Jeremiah the prophet was a sensitive soul, one who voiced the age-old complaint to God: *Why is this world such an unfair and unpleasant place?* God's reply: "If you have raced with men on foot, and they have wearied you, / how will you compete with horses?" (Jer. 12:5) To paraphrase: *If you are complaining now, how will you cope when things get even worse?*

One of the pleasures in reading the Scriptures is that we find more friends for the soul. Jeremiah is one, a fascinating man to know. He was good, moral, and sensitive, but one whose lament led God to say to him, in effect, "Toughen up, Jeremiah." Before the Book of Jeremiah ends, we see that the prophet really could "compete with horses."

In the 1800s Florence Nightingale became a world heroine for her tireless care for the sick and for reforming the profession of nursing. She wrote that "life is a hard fight, a struggle, a wrestling with the Principle of Evil, hand to hand, foot to foot. The night is given us to take breath, to pray, to drink deep at the fountain of power. The day is given to use the strength which has been given us, to go forth to work till the evening." Almost single-handedly she created modern nursing and made it efficient.

"Let us run with endurance the race that is set before us. . . . Lift your drooping hands and strengthen your weak knees" (Heb. 12:1, 12). Sometimes we need to hear those words and take them to heart, just as we hold dearly to these words: "Come to me, all who labor and are heavy laden, and I will give you rest" (Matt. 11:28).

Our strength, or God's? What a pointless question. What matters is remembering that there is surely more strength than we imagined, and in this fallen world we shall surely need it.

Resolution: Think of people you know who have surprised you with their toughness and grit during a crisis. Do you think they were self-reliant, or God-reliant, or perhaps both?

83

Dead Air

A fool takes no pleasure in understanding,
but only in expressing his opinion.

Proverbs 18:2

EDUCATION is a wonderful thing—so long as you are learning something worth knowing. Much of what passes for education these days is a waste of time. I rather enjoyed school, and thoroughly enjoyed my college years, and the most valuable thing I learned was that I had learned so little, that what I knew amounted to the tiny tip of an iceberg.

I also learned that teachers are human, and the desire to educate young minds is only one of their motivations. Many of them are deeply in love with the sounds of their own voices, and they enjoy having a captive audience. (Alas, this is true of many pastors also.) I have the greatest respect for dedicated, competent teachers—but none for those who went into teaching because they love getting paid for expressing their opinions all day. Near my home are Gulf beaches where vain people stand around in swimsuits, as if to say, "Look at me—I'm so beautiful." The schools are full of a different breed of egomaniacs, the "Look at me—I'm so smart" type.

Such people are not limited to the teaching profession. There are blowhards and chatterboxes everywhere—in your office, your neighborhood, Internet chat rooms, talk radio, the various "talking heads" shows on television, and so on. Some are genuinely intelligent, most not. All of them give the impression that they are not the least interested in altering their opinions, nor hearing someone else's, except to contradict them. Some of them show up on *Today* or *Oprah* in the role of "experts"—which is amusing, since no one can agree on who the "experts" are, including the authorities themselves. (Would TV producers really know an expert if they saw one?) Some of these shows have huge audiences, which makes one wonder: Are viewers wise enough to know that "experts," even with graduate degrees and good haircuts, might also be fools who delight in airing their opinions?

Proverbs 18:2 is paraphrased in the old rhyme about the wise old owl who lived in an oak: "The more he heard, the less he spoke, / The less he spoke, the more he heard." Put another way, you learn more by listening than by talking, and if you are talking constantly, you are probably not listening (or learning) at all. And remember that "fool" in the Book of Proverbs doesn't mean someone who is just mentally deficient, but morally lacking as well. While the chattering fool is entertaining some people (and boring others), he is neglecting his own moral growth, and perhaps harming other people as well.

The bottom line: control your own tongue, and be a skeptic in regard to the opinionated people of the world.

———

Resolution: Give yourself a day off from opinions. Turn off the talk radio and the talking heads shows on television, and scrap the editorial page of the newspaper. Absorb something worthwhile—say, the Bible.

84

Ill-Gotten Grain

People curse the man who hoards grain,
but blessing crowns him who is willing to sell.

Proverbs 11:26 (NIV)

ONE of the saintly heroes of the Old Testament is Joseph, the favorite of the twelve sons of the patriarch Jacob. Given a "coat of many colors" by his doting father, Jacob aroused his brothers' jealousy, so they sold him as a slave. Taken to Egypt, he managed—through wisdom, character, and the hand of God—to become the Pharaoh's right-hand man. When his brothers were starving because of a famine in Canaan, they journeyed to Egypt to buy grain, and whom did they encounter but their long-lost (and forgiving) brother Joseph . . . who sold them the grain they needed so desperately.

Joseph was such a beloved figure in Hebrew tradition that we can assume the author of Proverbs 11:26 had him in mind as the "blessed" person who was willing to sell. And though the verse does not say so, we can probably assume that "willing to sell" meant "willing to sell at a reasonable price." Surely price-gouging would be just as sinful as hoarding.

The Bible—and the Book of Proverbs in particular—has much to say about people who exploit others for gain. Proverbs 11:26 is obviously referring to people we would call "speculators"—people who buy up a supply of a commodity, then hoard it so as to produce a scarcity and (somewhere down the road) higher prices when they finally decide to sell.

During America's Civil War, Southerners became all too familiar with such loathsome characters. The Confederacy faced shortages of many necessities, and speculators, who had no qualms about buying and hoarding such essential items as salt, wheat, and nails, only worsened the situation. Confederate newspapers were relentless in condemning the wretches who happily exploited their fellow citizens. And while the citizens and newspapers wailed and cursed, the speculators grew rich.

The fictional Rhett Butler in *Gone with the Wind* made many enemies because his speculation allowed him to dress well and eat well while others went shoeless and hungry, and the South had plenty of real-life Rhett Butlers. When the novel *Gone with the Wind* was made into a movie, the scriptwriters chose not to mention that Rhett Butler had been a speculator, for fear that audiences would detest him. The historians still debate whether the war might have had a different outcome if the Confederacy had not suffered the financial manipulation of the speculators.

As long as human beings exist in this world, they will attempt to exploit each other for money. People of faith who deal in business have to ask themselves some obvious questions: *Am I charging too much for my goods or services? Would I be willing to let God audit my books? When I stand before a righteous God at the Last Judgment, is there anything in my business practices that will make me ashamed? Could* anyone ever accuse me of "leaving my faith outside the office door"?

Resolution: Do a _"spiritual business inventory,"_ taking stock of how you deal with people in the workplace. Are you fair and honest with employees, employers, and customers? Are you conscious, in the midst of your workday, that God is watching?

85

Sentimental Fools—
Bless 'Em

He who finds a wife finds a good thing
*and obtains favor from the L*ORD.

Proverbs 18:22

VALENTINE'S Day is the great holiday for adults. My great-grandfather taught me that. Long before I felt any stirrings of love or romance myself, Levi Carpenter showed me how they worked in a world of adult feelings.

Levi said it was special because it was also his anniversary. He had proposed to Great-Grandma Letitia—"Letty"—on New Year's Eve, and when she said yes, he said, "Pick a day, and make it one I can always remember." She chose February 14.

By the time I came into the world, Levi and his Valentine wife were well past sixty, but I saw that the day was special for them. Living only a few miles away, I saw them most every weekend, and without fail, every weekend after Valentine's Day a huge bouquet of pink roses graced the mahogany table in the foyer. And somewhere near the vase was Levi's one annual attempt at artistry: a large snow-flake, delicately cut from paper, a reminder that there had been snow on their wedding day. Attached to it was a note: "To Letty, my Valentine lady." The words never changed from year to year.

Yet the snowflakes always changed. Levi said no two were alike, and he made them all as different as nature did. At age nine I discovered a nook in the china cabinet where, laid away lovingly and tidily, was every anniversary snowflake, even the original one that said, "To Letty, my Valentine lady for a whole year." It was a curious thing that a man with such horrible handwriting could, just once each year, make his words spread across the paper like some lovely flowering vine. Levi was a carpenter who was widely considered tight-lipped and unemotional. And somehow he transformed a plain piece of white paper into a work of art, using nothing more complex than scissors and a pen, along with some deft folding.

The last snowflake Letty ever saw was inscribed, "To Letty, my Valentine lady these 56 years." The following year, Levi made his way to the cemetery on February 14. I saw Levi take something from his coat pocket and tuck it down inside the stone vase. It appeared to be a piece of paper.

A year later, Levi was there—buried beside the wife he had loved quietly and faithfully for more than half a century. When I visited the cemetery on February 14, I saw that Levi's last valentine was stuffed into the bottom of the stone vase on their double headstone.

Resolution: Talk to couples who have been married for fifty years or more. What made their marriages work?

86

Last House on the Right

In the house of the righteous there is much treasure,
but trouble befalls the income of the wicked.

Proverbs 15:6

"THE house of the righteous" would be a fine subtitle for the whole Book of Proverbs, and for that matter the goal of godly living could be summed up in the words "in the house of the righteous there is much treasure."

If you browse through Proverbs, you notice something called *parallelism*—one thing stands in stark contrast to another. Often the signal for parallelism is a "but," as in 15:6:

"In the house of the righteous there is much treasure, but
trouble befalls the income of the wicked."

Good thing (the righteous) versus bad thing (the wicked). Some other "but" passages: "He mocks proud mockers but gives grace to the humble." (3:34) "The wise inherit honor, but fools he holds up to shame." (3:35) Mentally, this is a great teaching tool, for contrast makes the words stick in the mind. The verse concerns money and possessions, which are not bad in themselves but can be foul in the hands of bad people. The righteous spend wisely and even use their wealth to aid the poor, but the wicked spend foolishly and bring trouble on themselves.

Proverbs 15:6 seems to say that the righteous will have wealth. Will they? Read a few verses further: "Better is a little with the fear of the LORD / than great treasure and trouble with it" (15:16). Or one verse further: "Better is a dinner of herbs where love is / than a fattened ox and hatred with it" (15:17). Is Proverbs contradicting itself? Not really. It reflects the multifaceted teaching of the Old Testament: God often blesses the righteous with worldly prosperity—but it is always better to be poor and good than rich and wicked. Wealth does not necessarily bring happiness or inner peace. "Whoever trusts in his riches will fall, / but the righteous will flourish like a green leaf" (11:28).

Of course, we have spiritualized the words "in the house of the righteous there is much treasure." We interpret "treasure" as spiritual riches, not worldly goods. If this was not the original meaning of the words (and we can't know for sure), it is certainly the meaning that hundreds of generations of the godly have read into it. Jesus told his followers to lay up for themselves "treasures in heaven" (Matt. 6:20), the only things that endure. He, and all who trust in him, surely understand the deepest meaning of Proverbs 15:6. Perhaps that proverb's original author, had he lived to Jesus' day, would have said, "Ah, I had in mind money and possessions when I wrote 'in the house of the righteous there is much treasure,' but I see now that there is infinitely greater blessing for the righteous than material things."

As the apostle Paul put it, we should strive to be "rich in good works" (1 Tim. 6:18). That, truly, is treasure in anyone's house.

Resolution: Think of people you know who are rich in the spiritual sense. What is their attitude toward material goods? Think of people you know who are rich in the material sense. Are they happy and content, or always wanting more than what they have already?

87

Omitting the Goats

Do not withhold good from those to whom it is due,
when it is in your power to do it.
Do not say to your neighbor, "Go, and come again,
tomorrow I will give it"—when you have it with you.

Proverbs 3:27–28

WE usually think of evil as something we do *to* people: lying to them, stealing from them, cheating on them, exploiting, abusing, or deceiving them in some way. Traditional church language called these "sins of commission." As you see in Proverbs 3:27–28, there are other forms of sin, what used to be called "sins of omission." We can *commit* sins, and we can *omit* doing good—which is also a sin. The traditional Church of England confession phrases it well: "We have left undone those things which we ought to have done, and we have done those things which we ought not to have done."

People tend to think of religion as a set of "do nots." On the *Tonight Show*, host Jay Leno took to the streets to see what people knew about the Ten Commandments. One woman fumbled for an answer and finally said, "Well, you know, they mean—they mean you can't do anything." Amusing—but not accurate. True, there are lots of things a godly person should avoid. But "you can't do anything" is not exactly a summary of Christian behavior. We can enjoy not just innocent pleasures (there are still plenty of those, thankfully) but do active good in the world. If we ignore the needy, we are guilty of "sins of omission."

Jesus had a lot to say about these sins. His parable of the Last Judgment (Matthew 25:31–46) shows how serious such failures can be. At the end of time, people will be separated into "sheep" and "goats"— the "goats" being the ones who neglected to help the Lord when he was sick or hungry or in prison. The goats are stunned: *When did we have the opportunity to come to your aid, Lord?* The famous reply: "As you did not do it to one of the least of these, you did not do it to me" (v. 45). The goats he consigns to "the eternal fire prepared for the devil and his angels" (v. 41). The "sheep," those who aided the needy, enter heaven. Clearly the Lord takes the sins of omission seriously.

Jesus understood an unpleasant reality: a person can be "religious" but not particularly compassionate. One can attend church regularly, pray, read the Bible, and avoid most kinds of sin—but still turn a deaf ear to people in need. That is what the "goats" did. They neglected basic human decency and missed heaven. Perhaps they thought "the eternal fire" was only for notorious sinners, such as murderers, thieves, and adulterers. Not so. Those lacking in simple compassion will be there also.

Not a comforting parable—and probably not intended to be. Jesus intended it to light a fire under complacent people, reminding them that the words of Proverbs 3:27–28 are not a suggestion but a command.

————

Resolution: Think of times in the past month when someone asked you for help but you declined. Why did you? Were you busy? Could you have spared the time and effort if you had been willing?

88

Legends in Their Own Minds

Do you see a man who is wise in his own eyes?
There is more hope for a fool than for him.

Proverbs 26:12

ONE of our recent presidents claimed he disliked "high-IQ dimwits," and anyone who has spent time around a college campus knows the type he meant. The schools are full of "educated fools," which is a very dangerous type of fool, quite blind to its own stupidity.

You can't read very far in the Book of Proverbs without bumping into the words "pride" and "proud." In our own day, being so mindful of appearance, we tend to associate pride with looks. We expect physically attractive persons to be vain (and they frequently are). You won't find such people in Proverbs, which connects pride more with money—and with mind. Apparently the authors of Proverbs encountered people who were arrogant because of their wealth or intelligence, not their looks. But pride is pride is pride—all of it sinful, in the Bible's view, because we make an idol of ourselves, and instead of worshiping God, believe we *are* God. And while God knows everything, no smart person does—but many think they do.

In my high school and college days I participated in "scholastic bowls," which used a quiz-show format, each school having a four-person team competing to answer questions quickly and correctly. I thoroughly enjoyed these, and most of the players we met from other schools were nice kids, bright, pleasant, reminders that *education* is, after all, the main goal of schools.

But there were some puffed-up egomaniacs among them, as self-infatuated as any school's homecoming queen or football star. Between rounds of the scholastic bowl, I heard one of the best players remarking to another kid that he was "a confirmed atheist," a science whiz, and an astronomy buff whose telescope had convinced him there was no God "out there." This was an amazing assumption for a seventeen-year-old. After all, to know that there is no God anywhere in reality, you'd have to know all reality—and you can do that only if you're God. A teenaged boy with a telescope might be wise, but not *that* wise. This young man claimed he planned to become a college professor, which meant he could pass on his wisdom (and his atheism, perhaps?) to impressionable students. I hope he changed his mind and entered another field—or, even better, changed his soul. It is pleasant to think of this man putting his great intelligence to work for the Lord.

God grants us many earthly pleasures. Looking at an attractive person is one. Conversing with an intelligent person is another. *Wow, she is so beautiful. Wow, he is so smart.* But nothing mars the person's beauty or intelligence like our awareness of an overweening pride. *Beautiful—but, boy, does she know it! Smart, yes—but seriously in love with himself.* It is well that God made us this way, intolerant of the overproud. It is one way we prove we were made in his image. What we dislike in others we should (let us hope and pray) rid our own selves of.

_____

Resolution: Give yourself a "pride exam." What are you most proud of in your life—looks, money, cleverness? Are you ever aware of disliking the pride of other people?

89

The Party Zone (Temporarily)

Whoever loves pleasure will be a poor man;
he who loves wine and oil will not be rich.

Proverbs 21:17

WHICH is harder—making money, or spending it wisely? Spending by itself is easy—and enjoyable. Spending *wisely* is difficult. Ask any lawyer who handles bankruptcy cases. Many people who have money distribute it foolishly, with little thought for tomorrow. The lawyer's offices and civil courts are filled with people who are gainfully employed and yet bankrupt—mostly due to their own foolish habits.

Could it be otherwise, in our advertising-saturated culture? When have you seen an ad saying "Don't spend!"? Every product or service is presented as necessary for a happy life—a cola, a taco, a mutual fund, a home, a health-club membership, whatever. And if you do not have the cash to buy it now, those magical pieces of plastic (credit cards, that is) can delay payment for a long time (though not forever).

Several years ago a young man bought the home next to mine and turned it into Party Central. I happened to know the house was already in mint condition, but the new owner proceeded to add outdoor lights, a recreation room, a pool enclosure, a state-of-the-art sound system, all new appliances in the kitchen (though the ones that were there were barely five years old). Within a year of moving in he bought a new (and expensive) car and took two Caribbean cruises and a trip to Europe. When he wasn't on vacation, he kept his pool filled with friends, who gladly accepted the free food and drinks.

None of this prodigality was immoral or foolish by itself—*if* he could afford it, that is. But the piper had to be paid eventually. One day I noticed a *For Sale* sign on his lawn. The house was already empty. I learned he had moved in with his parents, and I heard later he made no profit from the sale of the house, for his creditors got it all. He had lived in his house barely a year.

According to an old saying, a spendthrift is no man's enemy but his own. Certainly this young man's spending benefited numerous stores and businesses in our area. His stupidity with money helped keep the economy humming, even if it proved disastrous for his own personal economy.

I like to think that if he ever gets on his feet again financially, he will spend with more restraint, but I have my doubts. God endowed his creatures with brains, but it is not his fault if we fail to use them. He endowed us with mouths also, and if those mouths cannot learn to form the words "That's nice, but I can't really afford it," there is a price to pay.

Resolution: Think of people you know who have had to declare bankruptcy. Was it a result of financial setbacks like illness or accidents, or the result of wasteful spending? Do you think the wasteful spenders learned anything from their experience? Did you?

90

Auto-Honesty

Dishonest money dwindles away,
but he who gathers money little by little makes it grow.

Proverbs 13:11 (NIV)

AUTO mechanics have a reputation for being less than honest with their customers. I have known many who fit the stereotype. But I am happy to report that I know one who does not. Nick is co-owner of an auto repair shop with his brother-in-law, Al, who is not a Christian. "Al is a great guy, but he's ambitious, always wanting to buy something new for his family or add a room on the house," Nick says.

"Every day we're tempted to do what almost every auto mechanic does: suggest repairs that aren't necessary. It's so easy to spook people with stories of what could happen if their brakes fail, if a certain part isn't replaced right now. Women and older adults are particularly gullible about such things. Al justifies it this way: 'Whatever we replace or repair, it would have to be repaired *eventually*, so why not do it now?' But I can't accept that. On jobs that I supervise or handle myself, I insist that the customer get the straight truth. If there's a problem that doesn't need prompt attention, I tell them that.

"Some of our customers are well-off. It's standard practice to try to push these people for unnecessary repairs. The attitude is 'What the heck, they've got money to burn, why shouldn't I benefit from it?' But I don't want dishonest money going into my account. I can't go to church on Sundays and let greed rule me the rest of the week."

"Working for the Lord" (see Rom. 12:11 and Col. 3:23) must, of course, include working with integrity. Christians can serve God in the business world, on a factory assembly line, behind a broom handle or the wheel of a taxi. But wherever the Christian is, his work belongs to God. (See 1 Cor. 3:9, 10:31, 2 Cor. 9:6, Eph. 6:6–7, 1 Thess. 4:11–12.) There is no way we can please God while cheating or deceiving our fellow man.

We also can't please God by ignoring the Sabbath commandment. "My business partner often works on Sundays, doing repairs on cars that were left on Friday. He brings in more money that way, and he tells me I'm a fool for not doing the same. But I take the Sabbath seriously. It's a day of rest, the Lord's day, not another money-making day for me."

Nick has done well in his business. He could do better—by the world's standards—by practicing his business the way his partner does. He chooses not to. He says he would rather pinch pennies at home than pinch the pennies of his gullible customers. The author of Proverbs 13:11 would heartily approve.

Resolution: Seek out some Christians who have succeeded in the business world. Talk to them about how they maintain integrity in a world that places no high value on honesty.

91

Speaking in (Forked) Tongues

A gentle tongue is a tree of life,
but a perverseness in it breaks the spirit.

Proverbs 15:4

W HEN people were writing the Book of Proverbs, the times
were violent. This is why the book is filled with warnings
about associating with those who plot and perpetrate bloodshed.
Apparently life and blood were cheap in ancient days. But justice
was swift—if you committed a crime, you could expect quick
vengeance.

It is easy for us to pass over the verses in Proverbs that refer to violence. Most of us, in the course of our lives, will probably not commit brutal acts nor plot with others to do so. Any one of us could be
a *victim* of violence, of course, for terrorism is a threat that shows no
signs of going away. But for the person trying to live a moral life, actual bloodshed is probably not a daily temptation.

But Proverbs has plenty to say about the other form of violence,
the bloodless but destructive use of the tongue. The Bible's authors
may have lived in savage times, but they didn't neglect to speak of
the harm done by the abuse of the tongue.

You see this not only in Proverbs but in Psalms as well. The Psalms are full of warnings against "deceitful lips," lies that "cut like a razor," sneering and jeering, perjury, flattery, words that "wound like a sword." Apparently the ancient Hebrews inhabited the same spiritual universe that we do.

I recall spending summers with my grandmother, who was friends with a widow who was active in her church. During one of our visits, the old lady pointed out to my grandmother that she marked on her kitchen calendar the dates when girls she knew were married. When my grandmother asked why, the lady told her, "So when her first baby is born, I'll know if it took less than nine months." She also mentioned that once she confirmed that a certain girl "had to get married," she proceeded to call her friends to let them know.

In the great scheme of things, this wasn't a huge sin. But clearly she took some delight in spreading scandal. I wondered, since she never missed church on Sunday, had her pastor ever preached on the Bible's many condemnations of gossip and slander? Was she aware that every little action of the common day makes or unmakes character?

Where sins of the tongue are concerned, few of us are sinless. I delight in gossip as much as the next person—and so pray often that I will hear as little of it as possible. We should all heed the warning of Proverbs 15:4. When it says that a perverse tongue "breaks the spirit," it may be referring to the people it harms—and also to the possessor of the harmful tongue.

———

Resolution: Recall the figure of the "three wise monkeys," the ones that "hear no evil, see no evil, speak no evil." An old cliche, but one worth keeping in mind.

92

My Way, Even If It Kills Me

The way of a fool is right in his own eyes,
but a wise man listens to advice.

Proverbs 12:15

FRANK Sinatra boasted in song, "I did it my way," and that might well be the anthem of the modern world. A generation later, rocker John Mellencamp mocked the older and wiser in "The Authority Song." We could easily fill up a book by listing songs on the do-my-own-thing theme. Pop singers and songwriters seem to have a low opinion of authority and a high opinion of the individual's capacity to guide his own life. The theme has yielded some very singable songs, and some very fouled-up lives.

What a shame. As I said in the introduction, authority is a way of using the knowledge of some for the benefit of others. The mother who says to the toddler, "Don't touch the hot stove" is acting as an authority. She knows from experience what will happen, and she is trying to spare the toddler some grief. If the toddler mocks authority, he ends up with burnt fingers. When one's flesh is burning, "I did it my way" is not much consolation.

The father who tells his teenage son, "That rough crowd will get you into trouble," is speaking the truth. So is the mother who tells her daughter, "Boys will promise you practically anything to get sex." The adults know from experience—their own or others'. The kids don't, and their own experience can prove to be a costly teacher. The whole Book of Proverbs is the advice of a wise father (God, that is), trying to spare his children much grief in this fallen world. The wise pay attention, the fools go their own way, and suffer.

Of course, it's hard to argue with the pleasure of the moment. A teen undoubtedly enjoys his drunken binge, even if he makes a fool of himself and feels nauseous afterward. A man enjoys his adulterous romps, but afterward feels guilt or fears getting caught, or both. A woman enjoys spending lavishly on clothes and jewelry, even if it leads to financial strain and the neglect of her soul. Proverbs is not antipleasure. But it is full of reminders that the pleasures we chase after—wine, women, material goods—are not worthy goals. "The good life" as Proverbs presents it is simply a matter of being a good person, which pleases God and makes us (spiritually speaking) rich and beautiful.

If there were anywhere on earth a lasting pleasure other than God, we may be very sure that human beings in their long history would have found it by now. The authors of Proverbs knew this, and more than two thousand years later, the wise still know it. They know that freedom to do as we like is a pathetic joke if we use the freedom to pursue empty enchantments that hurt ourselves and others. To be truly free is to put oneself under the protective authority of God. Authority means having Someone we trust more than we trust ourselves.

———

Resolution: Think of some authority figure in your life—parent, teacher, mentor—whose advice helped keep you on the straight path and avoid grief. Give that person a thank-you call, or send a letter or e-mail.

93

Outhoping the Pagans

Hope deferred makes the heart sick,
but a desire fulfilled is a tree of life.

Proverbs 13:12

O H, what a beautiful morning!" So opens one of the best-loved American musicals, *Oklahoma!*, which has sent audiences home happy for more than fifty years.

Oscar Hammerstein, who penned the lyrics for *Oklahoma!* and a string of other musical classics, was an "up" person who derived pleasure (and profit) from sending theatergoers home with a spring in their steps. "I know the world is filled with troubles and many injustices. But reality is as beautiful as it is ugly. I think it is just as important to sing about beautiful mornings as it is to talk about slums. I just couldn't write anything without hope in it."

Neither could the various authors of the Bible. You won't find the word *optimism* in the Bible, but you find "hope" again and again. The ultimate hope is, of course, spending eternity in fellowship with God and other people of faith. In the earliest days of Christianity, this proved to be a world-changing hope. Historians believe that one of the key reasons Christianity triumphed over the old pagan religions was that the pagans had no expectation of a happy eternity, while the Christians believed it with all their hearts. Pagans anticipated an unhappy end, while the Christians had an endless hope.

Of course, Proverbs 13:12 has a wider application than just our hope of heaven. Earthly hopes matter as well, and we can suffer deep heartsickness when our desires are not fulfilled. We tend to blame God ("I wanted X so badly, why couldn't I have it?"), seldom stopping to ask the painfully obvious question: *Did I hope for the wrong things?* One of my college classmates has made his life miserable by constantly pursuing beautiful women. He is average in looks himself, and could probably find contentment with an average-looking woman, but he has spent most of his adult life frustrated. If he blames God, or fate, he is misdirecting his bitterness. He should blame his own unrealistic hopes.

One of the keys to the life of faith is that the hope of heaven puts everything else in perspective. We may hope for fame or riches or a beautiful spouse. Or more modestly, we may hope for a comfortable home and a devoted spouse. But the earthly hopes can't help but seem small next to the Grand Hope. If our earthbound dreams are deferred, and they often are, we need not suffer heartsickness permanently, for "a desire fulfilled is a tree of life," and that ultimate desire is heaven. "He has caused us to be born again to a living hope through the resurrection of Jesus Christ from the dead, to an inheritance that is imperishable, undefiled, and unfading" (1 Peter 1:3–4).

———

Resolution: Consider some long-held hopes of your own life. Did you get what you hoped for, and did it meet your expectations? If your hopes were frustrated, did you readjust your expectations, or suffer frustration?

94

Honk If You Love Showdowns

A fool shows his annoyance at once,
but a prudent man overlooks an insult.

Proverbs 12:16 (NIV)

GOD takes his time, while the devil always hurries." So runs an old proverb that is not in the Bible, though it fits perfectly. The devil is in a hurry, and so are devilish people.

Not long ago, on a street near my home, a truck passed me going way over the speed limit. As it happened, the frantic driver was ahead of me at the next stoplight, turning left as I was. The light turned green, and the truck did not move. *Great*, I thought. *This guy was in such a rush, now he won't even move.*

So I honked. The truck began turning left, as did I—then it stopped and began backing up (toward me, that is). If he was attempting to rattle me, he succeeded. He stopped barely an inch from my front bumper, then shifted and went forward again—as I sweated profusely. At the next light, same story: light turned green, he didn't move, but this time I did *not* honk. Finally he moved forward and I was soon relieved to make a right turn onto my own street.

End of story? Not quite. Seeing that I was turning, the driver stopped, backed up, and followed me home. I drove into my garage, he idled by the curb. Who knew what condition this driver was in? Drunk? Drugged? Or just furious because I had honked? He finally drove on down the street. For weeks I wondered if he might return sometime to vandalize my mailbox or do some other mischief.

Two fools were involved here: the truck's driver and myself. When he first roared past me on the street, I knew he was not exactly a calm, self-controlled individual. So when he would not move at the green light, I was foolish to honk at him. He was trying to provoke me, and he did. Considering the many deadly road-rage incidents, things could have turned out worse than they did.

Think of the many "special offers" that bombard us daily in advertisements. "You must act now!" "Limited time offer!" Most things in life are not that urgent. The advertisers know that their best customers are those who do not seriously think through a purchase before making it. The police and courts are also familiar with people who rush into something without thinking of the consequences. The driver in the truck rushing up the street could have killed someone. My own impatience at that truck idling at a green light could have led to a violent confrontation.

"A prudent man overlooks an insult." In the age of a thousand forms of unnecessary fury, how many prudent men are left? All the more reason to slow down, to behave more like God than the devil. *Pause. Hesitate. Overlook. Consider the consequences. Remember that the greatest remedy for anger is delay.*

Resolution: Pledge yourself to overlooking minor insults as you go through the day—while in your vehicle, at work, among family members, wherever.

95

Promises, Promises

*Train up a child in the way he should go;
even when he is old he will not depart from it.*

Proverbs 22:6

A PARK near my home is, on any given weekend or afternoon, a scene of family togetherness. Parents and children bike, skate, fish, sail model boats, and generally seem to enjoy each other's company. I am all for such wholesome recreation, but I wonder sometimes if the parents are neglecting the less-fun aspects of their tasks—such as teaching their children manners. Many of the kids are incredibly rude (and profane), and I seldom hear parents sounding firm and authoritative. Like me, those parents will have to live in a world where kids without courtesy grow into adults without much thought for others' feelings. The families give the impression that the dirtiest word in the language is *discipline.*

Proverbs doesn't say much about families enjoying each other. There was less leisure time in the ancient world, and parents saw their task as providing their children with food, clothing, shelter—and training for both work and getting along with God and other humans. If you did not teach your child how to live economically and spiritually, you had failed. Training a child involved setting boundaries and using the word *no* often. We can guess what the ancient Israelites would have thought of parents who make beer runs to the store to buy alcohol for their underaged kids' parties. So much affluence, so many expensive toys, so much fun—but what about the morals you are supposed to pass on to kids? What is going to happen when a generation of selfish, pleasure-seeking kids matures? Or will they ever mature at all?

All is not gloom. I do encounter decent, sensible, level headed kids who have some moral sense. I must assume their parents did something right. What puzzles me are the many other kids who were "brought up right"—but somehow turn out wrong anyway. What can parents do, except try hard and pray? We all know parents who did their best and mysteriously produced self-centered brats. I used to wonder if Proverbs 22:6 reflected badly on the whole Bible. If the Bible is inspired by God, then what went wrong with this promise in 22:6? We *wish* it were true that children brought up right will never depart from the path. We *know* that some do. Is Proverbs 22:6 an "inspiration glitch"?

One explanation, which I hope will suffice: 22:6 is not a *promise*, but a *principle*. We should bring up our children right and more often than not, they will turn out fine. Not always. But usually. And in any case, the mandate still stands: fathers and mothers are obligated to do their best at child-rearing, and that involves much more than providing toys and material comforts.

If they do so, and if their labors bear good fruit, they can take heart from Proverbs 23:24–25: "The father of the righteous will greatly rejoice; he who fathers a wise son will be glad in him. Let your father and mother be glad; let her who bore you rejoice."

Resolution: Think of families where children were raised right but turned out badly. Did the parents ever regret the way they had raised the children? Did they at least take some satisfaction in having done the best they could?

96

Beastly Behavior

A righteous man cares for the needs of his animal,
but the kindest acts of the wicked are cruel.

Proverbs 12:10 (NIV)

EVERY few years the news media bombard us with the story of the
latest serial killer, some demented person whom police finally
catch after he's killed several people, usually in brutal ways. I am not
sure how the public benefits from such stories, though they do fas-
cinate people. The chances of any of us actually meeting with a serial killer are probably slim, yet the evening news focuses on the
gory side of things, and apparently viewers respond.

One factor that often goes unnoticed: the killers usually started
their lives of crime at young ages—and before they brutalized
human beings, most of them brutalized animals. One example who
comes to mind is Jeffrey Dahmer, the Milwaukee man who was eventually sent to prison and murdered there. In conversations with Dahmer and people who knew him, investigators learned that in his
boyhood he began taking pleasure in torturing and then killing animals—both wild ones and pets. When his soul had become desen-
sitized toward the animals' agonies, he moved on to humans. He had

actually learned to take pleasure in the death throes of the creatures God made—first animals, then humans who were made in the image of God himself. First laughing at the final pitiful yelping of a stray dog, he came to laugh as he snuffed the life out of young men he met in a bar.

Proverbs 12:10 is one of the few verses in the Bible that speaks directly of kindness to animals. The ancient Hebrews did not have the sentimental view of animals that we have today. There were no animal-rights societies, and people thought of animals as either food or beasts of burden, not pets to cuddle and coddle. Still, you don't have to read far in the Bible to know that its human authors delighted in nature, just as fascinated as we are by the flight of birds, the swift movements of snakes, or the industriousness of ants.

There is actually just one mention of a pet in the Bible, and it is found in the story the prophet Nathan told to King David, the story of a poor man with "one little ewe lamb" that his family delighted in (see 2 Sam. 12:1–7). But we know from other verses of the Bible that people loved the beasts and birds, just as the God who made them loved them. In Genesis 1, God pronounced all created things "good," and we can assume the author of Genesis agreed. At the end of the Book of Job, God paints Job a vivid word picture of the wonder of created things—not only the stars and seas, but the mountain goats, donkeys, oxen, ostriches, horses, hawks, and eagles (see Job 38–41). Psalm 8 shows a respect and affection for the beasts of the earth. Jesus, a man who clearly loved the Galilean countryside in which he grew up, spoke of God's concern not only for people but for the ravens and sparrows (Matt. 10:29–31, Luke 12:24).

I had the good fortune to grow up in the country, surrounded by fields and forests, and I loved taking long walks in the woodlands, rich in wildlife. The downside of living in the country was this: people from the city often dumped their unwanted cats and dogs near us, and our home became an abandoned pet magnet. I can't fault my parents for showing tenderheartedness toward these beasts. If their original owners did not want them, they found themselves well fed and cared for by my family. I have to wonder about the people who abandoned their pets on a country road. Were they bad people? Were they as unkind to humans as they were to the pets that depended on them?

Resolution: I think of people you know who are deeply compassionate. Are they people who show kindness to animals as well as to humans?

97

Swords and Winter Winds

If anyone returns evil for good,
evil will not depart from his house.

Proverbs 17:13

INGRATITUDE is one of the nastier sins. Most of us, when we do something good to someone, expect him to return the favor—or at the very least, to *act* grateful. Certainly we don't expect bad deeds in return for good. If we are the hand that feeds and we get bitten, we are bitter. The Bible is, from one end to the other, filled with stories of ingratitude—man's ingratitude to God, and man's ingratitude to man. Forgive me if I quote a snippet of Shakespeare here: "Blow, blow thou winter wind, / Thou art not so unkind as man's ingratitude."

The textbook case of ingratitude followed by punishment comes, of course, from that colorful character, King David of Israel. On the whole, David was a good man—a passionate soul who loved God dearly and was loved in return. But his passions got him into trouble more than once, most famously in his infatuation for the lovely Bathsheba—who inconveniently happened to be married to one of David's military chieftains, Uriah.

You find the sordid story in 2 Samuel 11–12. David spied Bathsheba bathing, fell in love (or lust, perhaps), learned she was the wife of one of his captains, and arranged for the loyal Uriah to be placed on the front lines of the fighting. Uriah was killed, David married Bathsheba—who was already pregnant with his child. David was pleased: he had the woman he desired and no one (so he thought) suspected him of anything. David had forgotten that the God he loved so passionately had seen everything.

God sent the prophet Nathan to David, and Nathan promised him that "the sword shall never depart from your house" (2 Sam. 12:10). The child died, and more punishment followed as David and his many wives and children became a living illustration of *dysfunctional family*. David had to deal with his own painful case of ingratitude as his beloved (and spoiled) son, the handsome Absalom, plotted to take the throne from his father (2 Sam. 13–18). David nearly lost his life as well as his throne, and the rebellion ended in the death of Absalom, which broke David's heart.

Interestingly, Proverbs 17:13 is attributed to Solomon—who happened to be the son of David and Bathsheba. Was Solomon remembering all the sorrows visited upon his father's household? Perhaps so. Even after David's death, one of Solomon's many half brothers tried to claim the throne of Israel, resulting in a rebellion and his own death. Afterward Solomon enjoyed a peaceful reign, but after his death the family curse showed up again, as Israel split into two rival kingdoms.

What might have been spared David and his descendants had he controlled his lust for Bathsheba—and also remembered that she was the wife of one of his steadfast servants? We know little about Uriah, only that he was faithful to his master—and David paid back that fidelity by taking his wife and arranging for him to be killed in action. As Proverbs says, such heartless deeds do not go unpunished.

All of us are selfish by nature. Proverbs 17:13 is not addressing our "everyday" selfishness (which is bad enough) but the "advanced" selfishness of doing harm to those who have done us good. We all, from time to time, bite the hands that feed us—God's, our parents', many others'. Perhaps we ought to read the story of David and Uriah more often.

———

Resolution: Think of times in your own life when you have been un-grateful—or, at least, did not show sufficient gratitude for a kind-ness done to you. Consider calling or writing someone that you neglected to show that you were grateful.

98

Wounds and Kisses

An honest answer is like a kiss on the lips.

Proverbs 24:26 (NIV)

Faithful are the wounds of a friend;
profuse are the kisses of an enemy.

Proverbs 27:6

E VERY TV sitcom has at least one episode in which one of the main characters decides to be totally honest—and ends up turning all his friends into enemies. The message is comical, and clear: in our daily lives, being totally honest does not work. An honest answer is a slap in the face, not a kiss on the lips. Call it hypocrisy, or call it courtesy, but we make our own lives easier if we are not *too* honest with people.

Is this right? To a point, yes. If one of your coworkers wears something absolutely hideous (in your opinion, that is), you are under no Christian obligation to say how unsightly it is. Silence is a good option.

But what about those with whom we are emotionally close? Wouldn't honesty be a good thing? If a dear friend really does dress badly, so that you are aware of others snickering behind her back, it would be an act of compassion to tell her—gently, of course. On a deeper level, if a friend is polluting his life with drugs, alcohol, or sexual promiscuity, honesty is essential. Otherwise you are giving silent consent to a destructive behavior. To your friend's question, "You think I ought to end this extramarital affair?" the obvious answer is "Yes, definitely!" That is the right answer, even if it is the one your friend would rather not hear.

We live in an open society where we can pick and choose our friends—and our churches as well. We tend to select both on the basis of their saying nice things about us—and not saying things we would rather not hear. Pastors rely on contributions from people in the pews, and if those people are angry, they move on to another church. Thus the preacher in the pulpit can be as mealymouthed as our friends. You: "Do I look good in this outfit?" Friend: "Yes, you look great." You: "Should I stop living with my girlfriend and marry her?" Pastor: "Oh, I'd rather not talk about that. Let's talk about the love of God. . . ."

That last exchange is unlikely to happen. In many churches the pastors know which issues to speak about and which to avoid. A pastor may be aware that some of his church members are dishonest in their business dealings, unfaithful to their spouses, or notorious gossips. Some pastors will risk offending such people by telling them the truth. They have a great role model: in proclaiming the truth, Jesus had no qualms about offending people. Too many pastors—and friends—choose not to rock the boat. *Why be honest? I might lose a friend—or a contributor to our church.* More than we realize we have absorbed our culture's obsession with "tolerance" and not being "judgmental." Extreme truth-telling—in order to set someone on the right path, that is—is out of fashion. Perhaps that means that genuine love for others is out of fashion also.

"An honest answer is a kiss on the lips." "Faithful are the wounds of a friend." Still true, and like all true things, they endure and will outlast the shallow friendships in which people are criminally silent about their "friends'" immoral behavior.

———

Resolution: Think of times you were silent about a friend being on the wrong path, or even gave your approval. Was there some way you could have given your honest opinion without losing the friendship?

99

The Flip Side of Coolidge

A man of many companions may come to ruin,
but there is a friend who sticks closer than a brother.

Proverbs 18:24

Earlier in this book we looked at an underrated U.S. president, Calvin Coolidge—"Silent Cal"—a man of integrity, and also a man of few words. Let's turn now to his predecessor as president, a very different character, Warren G. Harding.

Harding was a textbook case of a smiling, backslapping politician. He was a chronic joiner, belonging to many clubs and making friends in all of them. A biographer wrote that Harding "was the familiar friend of everyone with whom he took a glass of champagne, and he took a glass of champagne with everyone." He was a genial, friendly, comfortable man—the flip side of his shy, reserved vice president, Coolidge.

But being everyone's friend has its price. If you make enough buddies, chances are some of them will be rotten. Many of Harding's were. Several of his top officials left office in disgrace. Historians remember him for hobnobbing with a nest of unethical men. Apparently he shared their contempt for marital fidelity, as he kept mistresses and fathered at least one illegitimate child. He loved late-night poker games and whiskey in the White House, even though Prohibition (which he had voted *for* in his Senate days) was in force. He was a handsome and charming party animal—and an immoral man with immoral friends. Only his untimely death saved him from political ruin. Happily, none of the Harding gang's "sewage" stuck to the honest Coolidge, who was choosier in his friendships.

Before Harding died, he lamented that his friends had brought him more grief than his enemies had. He could see that no one among his multitude of so-called pals had steered him on a wise and moral course. One wonders what might have happened had he mingled with people of integrity, like "the little fellow," as he called Coolidge. Certainly Coolidge benefited by *not* partying with the Harding gang.

Harding's own father claimed he was glad Warren had not been born a girl—for she would have been "in the family way" (pregnant, that is) all the time. Pa Harding realized his affable, eager-to-please son just "couldn't say no." When you "can't say no," you fraternize with greedy and corrupt people who want you to do them favors; and when you have the political power of the U.S. presidency at your disposal, you have all the makings of a disaster.

We could fill a book with stories of people whose bad choices of companions brought them to ruin. Sadly, a book about the friends who "stick closer than a brother" would be shorter, but at least more inspiring. We must learn our lessons where we can, both from the bad people and the good, the Hardings and the Coolidges of this world.

———

Resolution: Size up your own friendships. Are you socializing with people of integrity, or are you wasting time with people of low standards, people who are helping to lower your own standards? Do some honest evaluating, and maybe some "housecleaning" as well.

100

Great Pumpkin, Great Satan

It is not good to have zeal without knowledge,
nor to be hasty and miss the way.

Proverbs 19:2 (NIV)

OF the many characters in the well-loved comic strip *Peanuts*,
Linus is many people's favorite. His curious belief in "the
Great Pumpkin" amuses readers, as does his statement that "it really
doesn't matter what you believe, so long as you're sincere." The
words sound rather cute coming from a child. You would think
adults would know better, for we have seen plenty of evidence in our
lifetimes that what people believe *does* matter.

On September 11, 2001, the world got a very unpleasant glimpse
of the actions of people who genuinely believed America to be "the
Great Satan." Many people died, and America has never felt as secure since that day. The terrorists were sincere enough to give up
their own lives during their destructive mission. They had sincerity,
they had zeal, but "zeal without knowledge," for their knowledge of
"the Great Satan" was incomplete. With all its many faults, "the
Great Satan" is, by historic standards, still a wonderful place (as witnessed by the millions who prove it annually by immigrating here).

Several years ago actor-director Warren Beatty gave loving attention to his movie *Reds*, which told the story of American Communist John Reed, a supporter and propagandist of the Russian Revolution. Reared in a wealthy American family, Reed was a wide-eyed idealist—and also naive as could be about what would happen if a nation was ever established on Marxist principles. The movie depicts him and other American Communists in a flattering light. When the revolutionaries in Russia turned into tyrants, Reed and his friends became slightly disillusioned—but never for a moment were they repentant about their support for the revolution. They were sincere, and (so the movie suggests) their good intentions were what really mattered.

Now that the files of the former Soviet Union are open for public view, we are aware of the harm naive idealists like Reed did—people who tried to convince the world that the Russians were creating an earthly paradise. Reed had zeal—but little knowledge of human nature or of the fallacies built into Marxism. The Russians were only too happy to use Reed and his fellow stooges to spread their secular gospel around the world.

Beatty could have used his movie to teach the lesson of Proverbs 19:2. Instead, he used it to teach Linus's message: *beliefs don't matter so long as you're sincere.* Our intentions and our sincerity do count for something, in God's eyes. But so does our willingness to pause and ask, *Is this person / cause / movement really deserving of my support, or would it be wiser to find out more about it?* It is wonderful for our hearts to be in the right place, but not at the cost of shutting down the brain.

With all respect to the adorable, cuddly Linus, he was wrong. What we believe does matter, and sincerity is not enough. In deciding what person or idea or movement to support in this world, we can be "hasty and miss the way," giving our time and energy to a cause that can do great harm. It pays to "do our homework," find out all we can before devoting ourselves to anything—zeal accompanied by knowledge, as Proverbs 19:2 tells us.

———

Resolution: Think of causes or people you have supported in your life. Did you ever get disillusioned when you learned more about them? Before you devote time and money to a cause, do you check it out carefully to see what you are actually supporting?

Doubts and Toys and Envy

Let not your heart envy sinners,
but continue in the fear of the LORD *all the day.*
Surely there is a future,
and your hope will not be cut off.

Proverbs 23:17–18

A M I really fooling myself? Do I really know God? Is he basically good in his treatment of his children?

Then why am I such a failure, when I've given myself to him? I mean, I'm not really a failure, but many nonbelievers seem much more confident, much more successful than I am. Do I really have the message of life for these people?

Oh, God, are you alive and loving? Are you really working in my life?

Strange, despicable thoughts for a child of God to have—yet how many of us battle them? Sometimes these questions don't even rise to the level of conscious recognition. Very seldom do we express them verbally to anyone. We especially fear revealing them to another believer—after all, wouldn't that be admitting that we were slipping in our faith? Yet expressed or not, they gnaw at the center of our being, and great anxiety and turmoil result.

Is it possible for the believer to resolve his doubts in an honest, intelligent, convincing way? Since the Bible is our authority for truth and life, we should be able to find an answer in it. But how can the Bible help the doubting person? If we turn to a passage that tells us "Have faith in God," what do we do? Can we have faith in God when it's God himself that we are doubting? Using verses to deal with doubts can be simply another way of repression. The basic questions remain unanswered.

Many people in the Bible struggled with doubt. Psalm 73, attributed to a man named Asaph, is an exposure of a sensitive person's inner conflict. Asaph started out by affirming that God was good to the righteous. And yet . . . *why is it that bad people seem to prosper?* he asked. *The wicked seem to thrive, so what is the point of living a pure life?* Asaph wasn't the first person to be oppressed by these questions, and certainly not the last.

What did Asaph possess? Not great riches and material possessions—the "toys" in which so many unbelievers reveled. Not self-confidence. Not the praise of other men. But for Asaph, these things ceased to matter. He had something better, something eternal, a personal relationship with the living God. Having that, nothing else mattered.

So often does the success of unbelievers threaten and puzzle us that we stop praying and studying the Word. We feel that God won't accept us with our doubts, so we try to work out our own problems and present ourselves to him in full belief. Yet the God of the Bible is a patient God, one who does not mock the doubter. He takes the doubting person and sets him high enough to see the world and its toys and idols in the light of his eternal purposes. So we do not have to let our "hearts envy sinners."

Sinners work to acquire things that perish. Saints work to become like God, and be with God.

———

Resolution: Declare your life to be an "envy-free zone."

Epilogue:

Good-bye and Get to Work

Like a lame man's legs, which hang useless,
is a proverb in the mouth of fools.

Proverbs 26:7

DEAR Reader:

Thank you for persevering through this book. It has been my
pleasure to walk you through some of the most powerful proverbs.
I say "powerful" guardedly, for the Book of Proverbs is not meant to
be *studied* or *enjoyed* but *applied*. As an author, I cannot *make* you
apply them—nor can God, for that matter. Only you can do that,
and only then do they become truly powerful.

Proverbs is not a pretty or poetic book. It is useful, and that is
much more important. Proverbs can change lives—again, *if* people
use them in life.

In the New Testament, the counterpart to Proverbs is the brief
Letter of James, the eminently practical book with its famous statement that "faith by itself, if it does not have works, is dead" (2:17).
James and Proverbs both hammer home this point: your "religion"
and "spirituality" are of no consequence if they do not have practical consequences in the world. If you aren't doing good, and being
good, your so-called faith is no good. Even if you memorized the en-

tire Bible and could quote it aloud, it would not matter if you did not apply it to your own actions.

Jesus told his followers that the two basic rules were these: love God, and love your neighbor. James and Proverbs communicate that message, and make it clear that if you do not love your neighbor, you surely don't love God. Much of what passes for "religion" and "spirituality" is really just a distraction from those two fundamental tasks. So we attend church, serve on committees, sing in the choir, contribute money, and host bake sales. We pray, fast, attend Christian conferences, buy (and perhaps even read) religious books, listen to Christian CDs. But we all know, deep down in our pores, that we can do all these things and still fail at loving God and our neighbors. But we would rather build cathedrals, hold spirituality seminars, and devote hours to music programs than do the truly indispensable things. Cathedrals, or compassion? The Bible leaves no doubt about which really matters.

James told his readers, "Be doers of the word, and not hearers only, deceiving yourselves" (1:22). Likewise, Proverbs 26:7 states that wise words can be as useless as a crippled man's legs.

So, dear reader, shut up this book, and shut up Proverbs, and go prove yourselves "doers of the word." Remember that every little action of the common day makes or unmakes character. Guard your tongue, be generous to the needy, control your anger, free your heart from envy, be honest in your business dealings, be faithful to your spouse, choose your friends with care, invest wisely, pursue inner rather than outer beauty, generously utter compliments and soothing words, be thankful for what you have, exercise your own God-given common sense, but rely ultimately on the wisdom of God.

In short, put those proverbs to work.

Also by J. Stephen Lang from Warner Faith . . .

Talking Donkeys and Wheels of Fire: Bible Stories That Are Truly Bizarre!

Bestselling author J. Stephen Lang has collected some of the Bible's most outrageous stories into one fascinating volume that is both entertaining and enlightening. From the temporary insanity of King Nebuchadnezzar to tales of many-colored coats, magnificent wheels of fire, and the rape and retribution of Jacob's little-known daughter, *Talking Donkeys and Wheels of Fire* is packed with such heroic adventures and bizarre situations as would rival *The Lord of the Rings* and *Raiders of the Lost Ark*. J. Stephen Lang has made almost one hundred of the Bible's wildest stories even more fascinating by providing readers with additional trivia and interesting tie-in facts, proving that the Old and New Testaments have enough excitement for everyone—especially those who might think that reading the Bible is boring.

Look for other books in this inspiring series . . .

101 Most Powerful Prayers in the Bible
A guide to communicating with God—taught through an examination of the Bible's most powerful prayers.

101 Most Powerful Promises in the Bible
Simple Abundance meets *The Complete Book of Bible Promises* in this powerful and inspiring collection of God's promises, as referenced in the Bible.

101 Most Powerful Verses in the Bible
Through an examination of the Bible's most powerful verses, this installment in the *101 Most Powerful* series reminds us that we are not alone in the world.